CAN YOU TRUST US?
OF COURSE!

15 SUBSTANCE ABUSE
COUNSELORS TELL YOU THEIR
LIFE STORIES.

JANET GAYLE JETT

ISBN 0-7414-2564-5

Published by:

INFINITY PUBLISHING.COM

1094 New DeHaven Street, Suite 100
West Conshohocken, PA 19428-2713
Info@buybooksontheweb.com
www.buybooksontheweb.com
Toll-free (877) BUY BOOK
Local Phone (610) 941-9999
Fax (610) 941-9959

Printed in the United States of America

Printed on Recycled Paper

Published August 2005

In the grand tradition of Alcoholics Anonymous,
only first names are used in this book.

For Jenna, who, at age eleven, dedicated her first book to Great Aunt Janet and for Catherine, future Oscar-winning screenplay author.

In Memoriam

Mark P.

Erle

Lillian

George

Tom

Mark N.

Sheryl

Jack

Marge

Joe

Della

Charlie

Acknowledgments

My thanks go to Rica, Krista, Marty, Mike, Dawn, Deborah, Carsten, Patricia, LouAnne, Mira, Marie, Paul, Jolene, Joanie, and Angie. I am honored that you trusted me to tell your life-stories. I have tried very hard to tell them accurately—even with the cutting and editing of the extensive interviews you gave me. You are my heroes.

My high regard goes to all the substance abuse counselors in the chemical dependency field.

My admiration goes to all my classmates for your dedication to the "cause" and my thanks for your friendship.

My appreciation goes to Ruth, Garry, Jessica, Toni, Maureen, Setha, Martin, and Barbara, our outstanding faculty and staff. You made our two years together so rewarding and memorable.

My special thanks go to Judy, Sharon, and Elizabeth. You encouraged me and "critiqued" me." Without you, this book would never have been started or completed. How fortunate I am to have such great friends.

My grateful thanks go to my A.A. friends—especially those from the Saturday Morning Women's meeting. You are all my sponsors, and you started me on the road to recovery. I know you'll always be there if I need you.

My appreciation goes to all of my friends worldwide. You have enriched my life so much.

My love goes to all the wonderful staff and residents at Willamette Oaks who support me in all my endeavors.

My gratitude goes to Nena and all of the volunteer senior peer counselors. I am proud to be one of you.

Finally, my love and admiration go to my family. I cherish each of you. You have loved and encouraged me in all my dreams and imaginings—even when you thought I was crazy.

To the Reader

This book was conceived in the summer of 2000, just after I had received my acceptance into the Chemical Dependency Counselor Training Program at Lane Community College in Eugene, Oregon. I discussed the idea with my Eugene writers' critique group, led by my friend and mentor, Elizabeth. Everyone was enthusiastic.

The life stories of my classmates intrigued me. I wanted to retell all of them, but thirty-plus auto-biographies would be too many. But I'm happy I could include the ones in this book. I think you will begin to understand how ethical and how dedicated these people are to helping addicts and alcoholics stay clean and sober.

My classmates are idealistic, but not naive. They know that they have an overwhelming job. They are underpaid, overworked, and under appreciated.

Of course, there are a few rotten substance abuse counselors. I think, however, you'll find that most counselors in the chemical dependency field are ethical and compassionate. I've been impressed with their dedication and integrity.

I know my classmates are the best of the best. I've met many others in the field who are as dedicated. If you, a family member, or friends need assistance, do not hesitate to seek help from the professionals. They care!

Apologies and Explanations

I must apologize to my readers for the liberal use of five asterisks to substitute for names of people and places. The interviewees could not have talked so frankly if I had used names.

Only two people requested pseudonyms. Therefore, I have gone against the usual practice of indicating the first mention of an assumed name.

If you have questions or observations, please e-mail me at jettjg@carrollsweb.com.

CONTENTS

Please join us in a moment of silence for the
alcoholic and addict who still suffer.

THE PROGRAM

WE BEGIN

Lane Community College nestles in a beautiful setting in the northeast portion of Eugene, Oregon. Some think the buildings are ugly, but we can glance up into the hills and marvel at the fall colors. On this first day of classes, frantic students jockey for parking spaces or jump off a Lane Transit bus. We feel the excitement and energy as we scramble for our classrooms.

It's only September, but the drafty room in the apprentice building gives a hint of winter. Tension rises to an almost unbearable level as people file in. There are about thirty students, but not all will tell their stories. Marty, Mike, Krista, and Jolene will. So will Deborah, Jan, Joanie, Marie, and Angie.

THE PROGRAM

Why are we here? We've been accepted into the two-year Chemical Dependency Counselor Training Program, commonly known as the CD Program, CDCT Program, our Program, or the Program.

To secure our place, we had to follow all the usual requirements of transcripts and college testing. The CDCT Program demanded more depth. For those in *recovery, three references were required from people who could validate the applicant's claim that he'd been clean and sober for at least three years. All applicants had to request three character references from friends, co-workers, or employers. That was easy, but then came the letter of intent. It was a mini-autobiography.

How intensely we struggled with this intimidating prerequisite:

"How much should I reveal?"

"What can I leave out or gloss over?"

"This is agony. Is it worth it?"

Most of us ended up telling everything. Then we waited and waited for the decision of the Program faculty. Our self-talk ranged from the supremely confident, "Of course, I'll get in!" to "They'll never want me!"

Many applicants were refused, and we, the lucky ones who received acceptance, confess to immediate elation and then the nagging question surfaced, "Can I do this?"

THE FIRST DAY

A somewhat sterile classroom greets us. One intriguing poster asks, "What does an alcoholic look like?" and showcases photographs of diverse individuals. Another lists some "class rules." The tables, arranged in an open-ended rectangle with other student desks around the walls, give no hint of the arguments, passions, insights, satisfactions, miseries, and worries that will vibrate throughout the year.

Marty and Jan are the first to arrive. Jan is older, and Marty has a ring in her right eyebrow. They smile at each other and sit in the middle of the table facing the front of the room. The other students file in. Most are dressed in jeans and carry large backpacks. Many gulp coffee from plastic cups and gobble doughnuts or cinnamon rolls. A few nod to previous acquaintances.

Angie sits in the back row, her long hair hiding her face. Joanie bursts in, "Thank goodness, I'm not late!" Marie seems very young. Jolene and Deborah have enthusiastic smiles and slip quietly into empty places. Rica seems just a little nervous. Mike stands out because of his height. Paul doesn't join us until Wednesday, and we don't even notice Krista.

The room becomes deathly quiet. We drum our fingers and sneak sideways glances at each other. Silent worries circle in our minds:

"Where are the instructors?"

"What have I gotten myself into?"

"Wish I could smoke."

"He doesn't look very friendly."

"I'm cold."

Then they arrive: Ruth and Garry, our main instructors, the backbone of the Chemical Dependency Counselor Training Program. The two women amble to the front of the room. Garry has beautiful skin and a quiet elegance. Ruth is a short bundle of energy. Students straighten in their chairs and wait eagerly for either Ruth or Garry to speak. Each welcomes us and presents guidelines and expectations. Some students write furiously in their new notebooks. Others listen intently. All too soon, their introductions are over, and it's our turn.

"Please tell us about yourself. Give a little of your background, why you're here, and your expectations of the Program. Who wants to be first?" Ruth and Garry wait expectantly.

Eyes roll. Heavy sighs break the silence. No one speaks and the quiet returns. Then someone, unable to tolerate the stillness, talks, and we begin the long, slow, difficult, and emotional process of merging into a cohesive group.

We don't remember exactly what we said in those first introductions, but we think it happened this way. Krista didn't look up until she was finished. Mike's soothing voice helped us relax. Angie had been undecided until someone more advanced in the Program urged her to apply. Deborah loves her work in a care facility, but wants to try something new. Jolene worked in a camp for disturbed children until the facility required more advanced academic standards than she possesses. Marty jokes and makes us laugh. Joanie's hands are so expressive as she tells us about her young son. Marie's face turns bright red, but she speaks in slow measured words. Rica talks slowly, gets excited, and her German accent tumbles out. Jan rambles about her teaching experience.

Another silence descends. Ruth and Garry look quickly at each face and then smile at each other, and Ruth says, "Take a ten-minute break. The restrooms are down the hall to the left." Chairs bang, and we rush out the door. Some of us race to the restrooms, and others sprint outdoors for a cigarette.

We've just finished our first Forum. Our whole group will meet each Monday during the entire school year. On Mondays, we'll hear speakers or participate in counseling exercises. Sometimes we'll view a video. On Wednesdays, we'll split in half, and each group will assemble at different times.

Now it's time for "Theories of Counseling." This will be primarily a lecture class, although no class with Ruth is ever all lectures. She encourages questions and discussions and somehow covers the basic material. We gasp at the class syllabus. Are we expected to read this whole book? Thirteen long chapters from "Psychoanalytic Therapy Systems" to "Family Systems Therapy." Ruth tells great jokes, but we long for lunch. Stomachs growl by the time Ruth dismisses us. Again there is a rush for the restrooms or outside for a cigarette.

Our ears hurt from the noise in the cafeteria. We search for tables. Second-year students wave us to theirs. Three of these second-year students will share their life experiences with you: Red-haired Lou who rides her bicycle up the Thirtieth Street hill to school; Patricia, former model and actress who drives a round trip of one hundred-thirty miles from the coast; and Mira, soft-spoken but so warm and welcoming. We pepper these second-year students with questions, and they regale us with stories about each other and itemize our professors' idiosyncrasies. We laugh and get acquainted with all the people in the Program. This might not be so bad after all.

We're relaxed and confident as we stroll back to our classroom. We're ready for a nap, but it's not to be. "Counseling The Chemically Dependent Client 1" is our next hurdle. Almost immediately we're assigned in groups of three: a counselor, a client, and an observer. We're given hypothetical problems, and then we have mock counseling sessions. From the first, we're instructed to give confidentiality terms, use open-ended questions, and keep "ourselves" out of the session.

Even those who are already experienced in counseling or interviewing find this assignment difficult. Stress levels heighten as we critique our new friends and peers. Just when we think we're finished, we have to switch roles. Finally, we get a break.

Then comes "Alcohol: Use and Misuse." We moan: another thick book, ranging from ancient times right up to the present day. Our notebooks fill, and our fingers ache from unaccustomed note taking. Garry releases us a little early, and we gratefully leave for home or job—exhausted, overwhelmed, but highly stimulated.

THE REST OF THE WEEK

The next morning we stumble into the cafeteria for a quick cup of coffee and some companionship before our new class. Tentative friendships form, and people reveal more about their lives. Some of us are full-time students. Others attempt to combine school and jobs. The majority are older than the usual "just out of high school" freshmen, and many teeter on the high wire of school, jobs, *and* family.

We're a little more assured and at ease as we head for our next class, "Understanding Addictive Behavior." Most of us have intimate knowledge of addiction: our own addiction, a friend's addiction, or a family member's addiction. We're positive we understand all about addiction, but we will learn so much more.

We're all seated and apprehensive. Our instructor, Toni, nods to us as she walks to the front and reassembles the adjustable podium to fit her height. She unpacks her briefcase slowly and methodically. We don't know it, but she's as nervous as we are. The class goes smoothly. This is a shorter class day for most of us, but we're just as tired as we were on Monday.

The next morning, we assemble again in the cafeteria. The second-year students hint at the "ordeal" of our small group section of Forum. This is the most challenging class of the year, but also the most rewarding. We all agree that anything we reveal in the sessions will remain there, no discussing outside of the session. (Although I can't tell what my classmates or I divulge, I can explain how it works.)

We arrange the tables in a rectangle. Jessica, a tiny graduate student, is our facilitator. She sits in the middle of the front table. Others sit beside her, and the rest sit in the other parts of the rectangle—all facing each other. We can sit anywhere we want, but some will claim the same seats at each session. We each give a short check-in: our feelings, conflicts, successes, or worries. If we want more time after check-in, we can ask for it. We try to stay in the present.

This is not a therapy group, even though sometimes therapy happens. If our problems are outside of the group's expertise, we're encouraged to seek further counseling at the free, student-counseling center. We discuss everything in these Forum meetings. At the end of each session, we draw from a card deck with situation pictures and are asked to reveal what the situation conveys to us and how it applies to our life in the coming week.

Tears, angry shouts, slammed doors, and other outbursts happen regularly, but so do kind words, encouragement, understanding, and empathy. Some days we dread the class, but other days we can't wait to get started.

We learn to ask permission before offering our views. We try not to give advice or to ask so many questions that other members feel as if we're "interrogating" them. We gain a much better understanding of our own motivations and quirks and strive to accept those of our friends and classmates.

Thursday is the end of the school week for most of us, but a few ambitious students tackle a three-hour class on Friday, "Counseling The Criminal Addict." Ruth, our professor again, keeps us awake with her jokes and intriguing information. Somehow she makes dry statistics interesting. There are many students from other programs in this class, which enriches our own Program as we adjust to different viewpoints.

Now the week is over and our backpacks are heavy. As we trudge to our cars or the bus stop, we wonder if we'll be able to sustain the momentum of our first week.

WE REMEMBER OUR FIRST YEAR

FALL TERM

EXAMS

The leaves turned red and covered the ground. As is usual in Oregon, it rained. The days grew shorter. Disquiet and anxiety ruled our lives. Ruth's study guide was comprehensive and long. How could we ever remember all that detailed information? Garry's study guides were shorter and appeared simpler, but required just as much study and review. Toni preferred daily or weekly oral quizzes. Those weren't easier, just less of a concentrated jolt.

Many of us assembled in the cafeteria before an exam to review and contest our answers. Ruth never gave us trick questions, but we had to read carefully. Garry's multiple-choice questions were subtle and her essay questions even more so. We had to be careful not to spend our valuable test time giving the right answer to the wrong question. The room was always cold, and fingers shook. We shivered as we wrote. Afterwards, as do students everywhere, we gathered in the hall:

"What was your answer to twenty-five?"

"I did terrible."

"I'm going to flunk."

"I think I did pretty well."

"At least it's over."

PAPERS

Oh yes, we struggled with these. Many of us had never written a research paper and had to decide between the American Psychological Association (APA) style and the Modern Language Association (MLA) style. Bibliographies were a mystery to others. We waffled back and forth between our topics. These were only the individual assignments.

GROUP PROJECTS

One of the most important precepts of the Program was learning to work together. In the alcohol class, we had to design a ten-session unit for our clients centered on "Alcohol Education." Some groups clicked right away. Others couldn't manage to meet together. There were even a few who exchanged harsh words because they felt someone was not doing his share. These group assignments permeated our classes during the entire two years. We did learn to work together. As competitive as we were, we learned that helping each other led to greater understanding and superior accomplishment.

ROLE PLAYING

Over and over we split into those groups of three: counselor, client, and observer. We all had our favorite people to work with, but Ruth and Garry would never let us get away with that. Our groups changed with each hypothetical problem, and we all had to assume each role.

Some of us liked to play the counselor, some the client, and the observer didn't get off easily. Constant reminders swirled in our heads, and our mouths turned dry as we struggled to incorporate them:

"Critique each other's performance, but be tactful and accurate."

"Establish rapport and listen."

"Clients are more important than your own feelings or a desire to 'fix' them."

"Listen from the aspect of your clients. Don't impose your values and principles upon them."

"Create a structured interview, but stay flexible in deciding when to deviate from the agenda."

We pretended to be an ex-convict trying to stay clean and sober, a pregnant teenager who sees no future for her baby or herself, and a tough, swaggering youth who erects thick barriers. We learned from each other and thanked those who had been working in the field for sharing their experiences with us. Would we ever learn to do it all smoothly and professionally?

The days shortened. We grew weary. We rushed to complete our assignments and to study for finals. Tempers flared, feelings got crushed, but somehow we came to the last day of class and relaxed with potlucks on Monday with the large Forum group and again on Wednesday with our small group.

In the small Forum, Jessica, our coordinator, had us write our first names in decorative letters. Then she asked each of us to write something that we appreciated about each classmate on that individual's name paper. We still treasure those heartwarming comments.

Finals week was traumatic, but we said good-bye with hugs and a few tears. We needed the long break, but it was hard to say farewell to everyone. Fall term had been a challenge, and we'd made a triumphal finish.

WINTER TERM

Ice and fog turned the Thirtieth Street hill into a monstrous mountain. Commuting by Interstate-5 caused normally placid students to curse and rant. Most, however, were delighted to be back in school.

This term offered an extensive probe into the use and misuse of other drugs besides alcohol. Most of us didn't have a clue of what *dual diagnosis meant. This was our introduction to the world of the emotionally disturbed and mentally ill addicts who might become our clients.

As drug and alcohol counselors, we could not diagnose. However, we needed to be able to understand and recognize when to refer clients to other agencies or counselors. We learned how to work with these mental health professionals to coordinate our drug and alcohol treatment with their mental health priorities.

Forum continued, as did "Counseling The Chemically Dependent Client." We revealed more of our hopes and frustrations in Forum. Setha, a youth-addictions counselor, provided us with compassionate and revealing stories about teenage and elementary school alcoholics and drug addicts. The class on AIDS opened our eyes to the seriousness of this epidemic.

Our big assignments were doing mock assessments and video taping a short segment of one-on-one counseling with a class member. An assessment is the beginning of treatment for a client. It takes about an hour to administer. It covers everything from the first substance use to a program for eventual recovery.

Most of us enjoyed working on the assessments, but the videotaping—Yikes! The worst part was the agony of viewing ourselves on tape and listening to the critique by our classmates. How we squirmed in our seats as we struggled to appear confident and professional.

Dawn joined us in the Program. She'd been enrolled in the night classes, and Jessica had encouraged her to apply for the Program. She was very quiet at first, but then started to participate in class discussions and to join us at "our" table in the cafeteria.

SPRING TERM

The classroom turned warm, but now we had to endure the racket of construction outside our window. Buildings were being demolished to make way for a new "Students First" building.

"Multicultural Issues In CD Counseling" stretched our knowledge of the ethnic cultures of our prospective clients. Toni taught "Counseling The Chemically Addicted Family," driving home the thesis that the entire family must address any family member's addiction. Maureen arrived to initiate us into the professional way we were mandated to keep clinical records.

The large Forum changed. *"CO-OP" and interning were coming up in the summer and fall. Recruiters from different agencies came to speak to us. We were thrilled to find so many who had graduated from the CD Program and were now managers and supervisors at their agencies. Interns could be paid, but usually weren't. Internships often led to future employment.

We had to interview for internships, just as if we were applying for permanent employment. We stressed about "proper" attire, what papers to bring, and how to conceal our jitters. Some planned to start in the summer or in the fall. Six hundred hours of interning were required for graduation, but the state of Oregon requires one thousand hours for certification of drug and alcohol counselors.

WE REMEMBER OUR SECOND YEAR

FALL TERM

NEW EXPECTATIONS

Now we were the second-year students. We met the new, first-year students in the cafeteria and regaled them with stories about our professors' idiosyncrasies and our own fumbles. We hinted about the "ordeal" of Forum. How superior we felt—until classes started.

"Group Counseling" was excruciating because we each had to lead a group at least once and possibly twice. Gone were the protective barriers of the Forum tables and the comforting reality that Jessica was in charge. Chairs were arranged in circles. We were both physically and emotionally closer.

Our groups changed, and new personalities merged and adjusted to old alliances and different expectations. At least we were comfortable with Toni and felt we could make mistakes and still receive encouraging feedback.

In the "Ethics" class, we discovered the sticky situations that would confront us. Ruth cautioned us:

"Be diligent."

"If you have even a tiny doubt, consult your supervisor and other professionals."

"Avoid social relationships with clients."

"Keep confidentiality."

We had so many circumstances to consider that we felt guilty even though we hadn't even started our careers.

We met with Garry on Tuesday to discuss our internships. Most of us were really happy, but a few were angry and disheartened. The happy ones felt that they were valued and given responsibility. The angry and disheartened felt that they were ignored, given no responsibility, and even made to feel unwelcome.

Garry listened to the impassioned fuming of the unhappy interns and made on-site visits to help improve the situation. Sometimes the situation improved considerably after Garry's visit, but a few students applied and were accepted at another facility.

In November, we received word that several of our classmates had passed the *CADC 1 test. This test is in addition to the one thousand intern hours to acquire state certification. Our worries began again. Could we ever remember two year's worth of facts and statistics about, drugs, counseling theories, or ethics? But that was in the future; we had to concentrate on now.

WINTER TERM

Our classes were all meaningful and challenging, but the "Perinatal" class tugged at our heartstrings—three terms of learning how to work with parents before, during, and after pregnancy. We studied the stages of fetal development and the effect of a mother's drug or alcohol use on the fetus.

Strategies to help mothers deliver and nurture healthy babies were outlined. "Wrap-around help" is the ideal—young parents need to find jobs and decent places to live. Parenting classes and other social services are vital to producing a safe and happy family. So much of this seemed obvious to us, yet we knew we would have to be the front-runners in assisting parents and children.

Maureen introduced us to "Crisis Intervention." Most days in our work with substance abuse clients would proceed quietly, but we must always be attuned to possible explosive situations. Could we stay calm and diffuse the situation?

SPRING TERM

The class, "Gender Issues" created loud and passionate discussions. Toni smiled benignly and urged us to speak out. Did any opinions change? It's hard to say, but again a new level of understanding and tolerance emerged.

Martin, a retired, psychology professor, taught our class, "Advanced Group Counseling." He'd mentored Ruth and Toni, and many of the counseling techniques that we practiced originated with him. We had to critique our own effectiveness as facilitator and also those of the other students. As Martin returned papers, two of his comments stood out. "You're too hard on yourselves." and "I can tell you're all good friends."

During this time, Lane Community College was facing a horrendous budget crisis for the next year. Programs were slashed, and ours was axed and eliminated. Protests and meetings did not affect or change this decision.

A great sadness descended on our class. With heavy hearts, we finished our finals and prepared for graduation. The real world beckoned, and more questions surfaced.

"What would we find?"

"Would we become burned out?"

"Should we continue on to a Bachelor's Degree?"

"Would we find the satisfaction and the feeling that comes from a job well done?"

OUR STORIES

RICA'S STORY

Cafeteria, Lane Community College, Eugene, Oregon, Spring 2002

I didn't believe Rica when she told me she was forty-four. I thought she was much younger than that, but the ages of her two sons convinced me that maybe she was. We had good times together, and I was impressed with her ability to get our projects and papers completed way ahead of the due date. Rica was the first person I interviewed. I was more nervous than she. Actually, we had two interviews, so I have combined them. Rica had a long round trip to get to school.

A graduate of the Chemical Dependency Program runs a substance abuse rehabilitation clinic near her home. Rica started interning there in the spring of 2001 and was soon hired. She passed her CADC 1 test shortly before this interview.

Rica grew up in Germany. At one time she was an apprentice for a wine company in Germany. Drinking was a social thing for her, but in her teens the drinking increased as a rebellion against strict rules.

"I'm not in recovery, so I don't have addiction, at least not to anything illegal. I do smoke, which is a big addiction.

"A main influence on my life was probably my family. We were really close. We still are, even though I haven't seen them a lot, but we have contact all the time. The way I was raised was pretty strict with a lot of family rules.

"That's probably why I turned into a tomboy. I was just against everything my parents wanted for me. They wanted this cute little girl, and I was this rough little girl. That influenced me. I didn't have a brother, and I wanted a brother really bad because I could relate to boys a lot more than to girls. Yeah, I think my family would be the one that I felt had the greatest influence on my life.

"My grandfather on my mother's side was an alcoholic. He worked in construction, and by ten o'clock in the morning, he'd had enough to drink where he'd—you could consider it as past the legal limit. He was a real nice guy when he was sober, but when he was drunk, he was mean.

"I remember this from when I was a little girl. They lived upstairs. We lived downstairs. We stood on the staircase saying, 'Grandfather, don't yell at Grandma!' and 'Don't destroy the kitchen again!' Things like that stick in your mind. But he quit drinking in his early fifties and quit smoking because of health reasons. From then on, he was the greatest grandfather anybody could have. We went for long walks and did a lot together.

"The second person in my life was my oldest sister who lives in Arizona. She emigrated shortly after I did. In her teenage years, she was quite a wreck. She drank a lot. She drank to get drunk. She hung out with all the wrong people, and it took her into her probably thirties before she gave that up. She didn't have a very productive life, but in the last ten years, she's been going to the University of Arizona. And it seems like she's a career student.

"A lot of my friends died in accidents while they were under the influence. I have two friends who overdosed with drugs, and I have just been surrounded a lot by drugs."

Rica had told us that she had been a rebel. I asked her to elaborate on her teen years.

"Oh my God, I climbed out of the window when I was thirteen to go to the 'back-then' disco and came home when I was supposed to. Then I'd climb out and do it again. I'd hang out with the guys with motorcycles, and my parents didn't like it. After awhile, nobody in town liked it either, but I didn't care. I had fun. I married one of them, and I'm still married."

When I asked Rica how she'd met her husband and what made them decide to marry, she hesitated, rolled her eyes, and said, "Who knows? I don't know. We met at a carnival. He was drunk. I was half-drunk. We met and sat together and met again the next day. A few months later, he went into the navy.

"The German navy, and I figured I'd never see him again. So I started dating someone else, but he didn't know it. And he asked me to marry him. So I did. I think we dated a year all together before we got married.

"My parents wanted me to have a big wedding, but first, we got married at the justice of the peace and figured that was enough for us. A whole year later, my parents did a real wedding in church. I didn't want to get married in church. I didn't see any sense in that. I just didn't agree with a lot of stuff. That doesn't mean I don't believe in God. I just don't believe in this bullshit that they dish up."

I asked Rica to tell me a little about her early days in America.

"Right, my husband and I lived in Germany our whole lives. Our older son, at the time of our immigration, was two years old. We decided we could make a great living in the United States. We didn't really speak the language or anything, but it was an adventure. We packed our stuff, sold everything we couldn't take, and landed on 20 August 1982 at Los Angeles International Airport.

"We had no idea what we were going to do. We didn't speak the language, as I said before, and had about fifteen hundred dollars on us. We spent a big chunk of that for the first few days in a motel before we found a place to rent. At first we lived with some friends, so it was quite an adventure. People do take advantage of you when you don't speak the language. But it's been twenty years and I'm glad we did it. I love it here.

"I cleaned houses, didn't speak the language, but they paid me a few bucks. We ate a lot of peanut butter and jelly sandwiches for a whole year. Nothing but! But it doesn't matter; you get over it."

One of the questions I asked almost every interviewee was what had attracted them to the field of chemical dependency. Rica answered this way.

"I worked as a secretary for a few years and missed the people contact. I like to be with people and even though I worked, talking on the phone isn't the same. My friends have always come to me for advice for whatever I could do for them. I don't ever turn them down unless it's totally impossible.

"The big reason for me to get into the field (the chemical dependency field) was I live in a small town where a lot of teenagers are on drugs. Drugs, alcohol, huffing, you name it. Some of these kids would come to my house. They were friends with my older son. I've seen so much pain in their lives. I thought maybe I could make a difference."

Another question that I asked was what her first impressions of the Program were.

"Oh, I wanted to back out right away. I thought, 'God, what am I getting into!' I wanted to leave."

I asked her if she picked out people that made her think, "My gosh, what are they doing here?"

"I did. I really did. I wondered about some of these people. How are they going to manage? Whether they were ready to or not to help other people make decisions that affect their lives so directly. Yeah, I did wonder about that, but I wondered about myself too. No, not scared, not terrified, just struggling to decide whether I was crazy or not."

We then discussed how her impressions had changed since that first day.

"They started changing quickly, because I got so much inside, deep inside, into everything within the chemical dependency field, the dual diagnosis clients, just all the aspects of it—you know—people's lives, different cultures. It's such a big field that I didn't see that at first. You know to me, just like most other people, a drunk was a guy who was lying in the corner. I know better now. So my life has changed a lot because of these classes."

Rica acknowledged that she felt very close to the people in our classes. I asked her if she could tell me why.

"I admire everyone, who goes through a program like this, sticks with it, works in the field, does internships, goes to school, and still are enthusiastic about their jobs and what they're doing.

"I got to be friends with a lot of my classmates. I know that when I'm done here in June, I'm going to miss them. I'm going to miss my instructors too, especially Ruth. If it hadn't been for Ruth, I think I would have dropped out after the first semester. I think that when I graduate, I'm going to say that. When I do the walk, I'm going to tell her. She kept me pretty much from quitting early on, not so much quitting the field, but quitting school."

Rica then mentioned the other option for getting into a rehabilitation facility's training service. Most rehabilitation facilities have their own educational curriculum, and the state also provides seminars to fulfill the minimum requirements for state and national certification.

"I could have done just an internship, but then I decided that I was getting so much more with this Program than by just doing an internship."

I asked Rica what was the hardest thing about the Program. We also talked about the language barrier she faced with English as her second language.

"The hardest part for me was going back to school after twenty-seven years. A lot of things were hard for me. I grew up agreeing with a lot of things that we were taught, but were hard for me to follow.

"The language barrier? Yeah, I read and write pretty well. I have no problems with that, I did two English classes and aced them. So for me, not having studied English in my early schooling, acing those classes was a big accomplishment.

"What I do have problems with is sometimes to say exactly what I mean. That is a language barrier. It still exists for me. After twenty years, I know exactly what I want to say, but it doesn't always come out that way. I noticed that happens to other people who don't have language barriers, so I don't feel too bad about it."

Rica and I then switched to the most valuable thing she gained from the Program.

"In the whole Program? That's really hard because there have been so many rewarding things. I can't even start to name them. It's just so valuable for me, whether or not I continue to work in the field. It's changed my life quite a bit. I look at things so much differently now."

Spirituality is an important part of most recovery programs. I asked Rica what she thought about the spiritual development of her clients in recovery.

"Ah, spiritual development. I don't know how I'm going to answer that one. I was raised Catholic, went to church all the time, don't go to church much anymore. I believe in God, and I think spirituality is great, especially in recovery. We all have a higher power regardless of what it is or what it means to us. I agree to that and think spirituality is most definitely a big part of recovery."

Rica had talked about adopting foster children and working on a Native American reservation. She felt that it would be perfect for both her and her husband. She would do the counseling, and he could take care of the maintenance needs.

"I'm going to go do some research, and I want to go over there and look. They have a new clinic where my office would be, so it might not be a bad thing. Instead of counseling a few people; I'd be counseling a whole town. My God!"

We discussed the many things that opened for her because of the program.

"I never would have had the chance to get a job at the reservation. Any job in the field would have been impossible. But you know what? It's funny. Last night, a friend of mine said, 'When my husband and I got a divorce years ago, you helped me through it. I told you back then you should be a counselor, and you laughed at me. And now you are a counselor.' So maybe some things are supposed to be."

I asked Rica, "Are you going to stay in the field now that you've passed the national certification test?" She replied in the affirmative, and I asked her if she could tell me her reasons.

"Yes, I can because I've had many jobs in my life and have never felt so much value. My job has value. I don't just shove paperwork around anymore or take orders over the phone. I'm dealing with real people. I make a difference. I know it works because I've seen it, and that gives me an immense satisfaction to know that.

"What keeps me in the field? It might sound crazy, but I really do like people. And I know I can't help them all, but if I can help some, then it's worth my while. It's really a great job. I like to go to work in the morning. I don't procrastinate or call in sick when I'm not. I just really enjoy being a counselor.

"A year from now, oh boy, a year from now? I'm going to be studying for my *CADC 2, my case study, and the 250 questions. That's where I'll be. But I'll be working in the same place. I don't have plans to change that. Neither do the people I work for. I fit in. As my boss puts it, I'm not a 'cookie-cutter counselor.' That's not what he wants.

"No, the paperwork doesn't bother me. When it comes to that, I'm really organized. I did that all my life, but the most enjoyment is the people—helping and working with them and seeing that they can change their lives. I've thought about that a lot of times. They come in, and I want to give up. But I take time and help them get there. That is great."

Rica has said that she wanted to work with teenagers, but she is working with young adults. I asked her about that.

"I work with adult, corrections clients, but you know what? They might be over twenty or even in their thirties. I have a twenty-three year-old son and seventeen year-old-son, and when I compare their teen behavior with some of my clients' behavior, there isn't that much difference. It's as if once my clients started to abuse drugs, they got stuck at that phase in their lives.

"That's what it feels like to me, and once they sober up, that's where they have to start out again, so a lot of times I encourage them. 'Go back to school. Get a *GED. Do something!' And they can and they do, so I don't think there is much difference in dealing with teenagers. A lot of my clients are between twenty-two and thirty, and a lot of times I feel I'm dealing with teenagers again."

Rica had just stopped smoking, so I had to ask her about that.

"Seven days! Seven days! I'm a little nervous, fidgety, but—seven days. Last night, in-group, my girls, my clients surprised me. They brought me flowers. I was so—I cried. Oh, my God! I'm helping them stay away from drugs, and here I quit smoking. They made such a big fuss and brought flowers. It was just amazing."

For my final question, I inquired if she had anything to say before I turned the recorder off.

"Um, hmm, let me see now. I'm really disappointed about our Program being cut. I think that anything that has such impact, such direct impact on the community should not be cut. With so many teenagers addicted, I think it's irresponsible to cut our Program.

"I know from my own experience that this Program is valuable for new counselors and for people who want to be counselors. Even if you do an internship in an agency, you will get a lot of information, but you will not get that depth, that deep insight into all the relations, all the related aspects of addiction that this Program provides. It's a big shame to cut this Program, and I thought I would let you know and put that in this interview. We shouldn't cut life strings."

MARTY'S STORY

Cafeteria, Lane Community College, Eugene, Oregon, Spring 2002

Marty sat next to me for our entire first year. I was much impressed with her organized binder. It was even color-coded. She cracked jokes a lot, and when I was overcome with silent laughter, our instructor looked at me. We had good times together.

Marty was an excellent student, but when we were taking multiple-choice tests, she'd change her answers at the last minute. I could see her erasing from the corner of my eye, and I wanted to give her a poke, but of course, I didn't. She finally became confident enough to stick with her first answer.

My first question was about the presence of alcohol and drugs in her childhood.

"It was always there! The alcohol. That's all I noticed. Everything else was covert. My siblings used mostly alcohol until we got older.

"Then came the drugs—pot, coke, and pills—they pretty much stopped at meth. That's where my siblings maintained their use."

I asked Marty about her school memories.

"I loved school. I was always active in school and sports, so that kept me occupied and not into the party scene. I wasn't a 'party' type. I was more the loner in the elementary school period. When I got into high school, I was more the class clown. I didn't have any real close friendships or relationships even though I was into sports, which elevated my 'status' in the school.

"Like a lot of other schools, we got tested or could have been tested for substance use in order to play on the sports team, but I didn't have any interest in using. I loved the sports, loved them. Of course, we lived in a small town, so that's all there was to do. Oh God! It was a one-stoplight town, and the stoplight only flashed yellow."

I then asked Marty what she did when she finished high school.

"The day after I graduated, I literally moved out of state with my older sister in Oregon. She was living there with her husband, and she encouraged me to move out of the small town and go live with her.

"It was another tiny, pitiful, little town in the eastern side of the state. I went from small town to small town and didn't really do anything. I worked, and that's when I started drinking and partying because the people I was working with did. That seemed to be all there was to do."

I asked Marty what type of work she did in that period.

"I worked in a mushroom plant. I picked mushrooms for a year-and-a-half, almost two years. I loved it! Actually it was fun. I worked with a lot of nice people. And I still love mushrooms and eat them all the time. The smell wasn't too great. Manure for a year-and-a-half, but it was fun. I liked it. It was different. I was eighteen and living on my own supporting myself. How much better can it get than that? My own place . . ."

Marty then explained to me that in Oregon, the legal drinking age was twenty-one, but in Idaho, it was nineteen.

"I lived very close to the border, so some of the people I worked with encouraged me to get my ID, so we could go to Idaho and go drinking 'cause you only had to be nineteen.

"This was where the funny part was. I'd gone to the DMV to get my ID. They screwed up my birthday. Instead of nineteen, they made me twenty-three. So 'Woo-hoo' for me.

I was only nineteen and now I was drinking anywhere I wanted. I was drinking all over the place.

"My friends were so jealous, and I was like, 'Woo-hoo! Look at it, man! I'm twenty-three!' So yeah, I was drinking in Idaho and drinking in Nevada. So I was like all, 'Woo-hoo!' This was good and I partied my ass off for a long time. When I actually did turn twenty-one, it was no big deal. I didn't have anything to look forward to like we're supposed to when we're twenty-one. I was already doing it.

"So I lived there for a while and then moved again to Nevada, worked in a little store, and then worked as a security guard in a casino for four years."

I commented that working at a casino, as a security guard must have been a different experience.

"It was different. It was crazy, though. There's some weird stuff that happens there, I worked the graveyard shift for four years. Along with that came the gambling, the drinking, and the paycheck. I was making REALLY good money 'cause they take very good care of their employees.

"On the other hand, they also provided free liquor twenty-four hours a day—not just for the guests at the casino, but also for the employees. I got free drink coupons when I cashed my paycheck there at the casino. That helped contribute to me putting those paychecks back into the slot machines and just getting ripped every day after shift.

"There were a lot of people—including me—who would stay there just to get drunk and hang out with people and then go back home. And that's legal. So I go back home and then to work—a vicious cycle. Four years of that."

I asked Marty what turned her around.

"Lost my job at the casino. Well, I shouldn't say I lost it. I got fired for some-not-too-good activities, all messed up with illegalities. In between all this other stuff, there was a series of screwed-up, bad relationships. At the same time that I was dealing with the legal sanctions and my discharge from the casino, I got my first *DUI. It was pretty sad when I—pretty funny now I look back on it.

"So I was, needless to say, stressed! I was panicked. I got evicted from my apartment because I wasn't working and just a whole snowball. Everything that you could think of—it's like karma came back around to bite me in the ass for all the other stuff.

"Then my parents ended up moving over to Baker City, Oregon, and they talked me into moving over there. Everyone follows the parents, which is a natural progression for my family. So I followed them and wound up living there again. I did some motel managing, and my older sister talked me into moving to Salem where she was living with her new husband.

"So I moved over there, worked for awhile, started school, met someone in Eugene, and ended up moving to Eugene. I've been here ever since. That was in 1993. I took the 'Addictions Counseling' class in Salem."

I asked Marty why she chose that class. What drew her to the subject and how did it relate to her family?

"It was because of my siblings—there's five children from my mother. My dad had three sons, so I have three stepbrothers. In all, there are eight of us. Seven of us grew up together. My youngest brother's biological father abducted him when he was two, so he didn't grow up with us. That's a whole Jerry Springer episode right there.

"My eldest sister and my three stepbrothers were heavy partiers: alcohol, pot, coke, and meth. Through the course of growing up with them and seeing what they were doing and going through is what swayed me into this field. I wanted a better understanding, and, granted, I was partying at that time, but I hadn't gotten into anything heavier than pot smoking. I went through that phase and stayed stoned for about three months when I was twenty, twenty-two and it was like, 'Why am I doing this?' And I just quit.

"But in the course of all that, my siblings were getting married and having children—or not getting married and having children. My oldest sister had four children from three different men, pretty much in rapid-fire sequence. She just had them, like boom, boom, boom, boom.

"At the time, she'd been drinking alcohol and using drugs. Her four children have all gone through a horrendous, horrendous, life—her not being there. I lived with them off and on for years, raising the kids. Usually she wasn't there because she was partying. The kids turned out to be heroin addicts, alcoholics, drug users, and they all were still in their teens."

I commented on how young all her nieces and nephews were.

"Yeah, they're still all very young. My seventeen year-old niece just had a child. She's managed to turn herself around. My relationship with this niece has strengthened. We talk a lot, and she's doing real well now. I've tried to keep in close contact with the kids, 'cause we've always had such an intimate relationship.

"One of the sixteen year-old boys joined the Job Corps. He was using heroin, injecting heroin, to be specific, so I hope he's straightening himself out. I'm sure the youngest boy is a *fetal alcohol effected child. He doesn't have—he has some of the physical characteristics, but mostly it's cognitive. He has numerous, cognitive disorders, and I'm sure that's what it is. The eldest is still struggling to figure out and find his place, but he's still using and is in a pretty bad situation.

"So I guess my desire to get into this field was fueled by my nieces and nephews. That's why I'm working with teens and will continue to work with teens with addiction issues."

I'd heard Marty speak of her first relationship when she came to Eugene. I asked if she'd be willing to talk about it. She agreed, but pointed out that alcohol is also a drug. Then she started this part of her life story.

"Yeah, we met at the bar. The people we hung out with were drinkers and/or pot smokers. And they still are. The majority of time when most of those people get together, the purpose is to get drunk or to get high. And they're the same age level as my ex and me.

"But, yeah we met in the bar, we drank. From what I remember of the relationship, it was fine. We didn't have any problems. We never even fought. Maybe that was a red flag right there, but that relationship ended.

"I guess she met someone else. Well, she already knew someone else. They ended up having an affair, and that ended ours after two-and-a-half years together. So the breakup wasn't due to any substance abuse. It was, I don't know how she wants to rationalize it, but the affair ended it.

"Coincidentally, my present partner, and I met at the club too, but she's not a drinker. When it comes to relationships in this society and being gay, the club's the only place to meet people, but on the down side of that, most people who go there are barflies and people with drinking problems.

"So more things became clear to me. As I went through this Program, I learned more about myself. So I think we always see these things, but we're not willing to accept them.

"But the people I hung around with when I first moved here are not the people I hang around with now. So I changed those people, places, and playthings. We still talk with them. They say, 'Let's go to the bar.' I have no desire to do that. I'm so phased out of it. There's no interest even though I still drink once in a while at home.

"Once in awhile, ***** and I will go out just to see what's going on, but I don't get drunk. When we go out, it's just a reminder of why we don't go out. It's the same people and the same dramas, so you—what was the original question?

"Yeah, this interview will definitely—oh, I don't care. Everything I've said about people here, I've said to their face. My family knows what I think?"

I asked Marty how she found out about the Program.

"When I was taking the alcohol and drug course, I heard about it. I kept telling myself that I was going to be a counselor. I wanted to be a counselor, but financially I couldn't afford to go to school.

"I was working for a carpentry factory at the time, making furniture and stuff, and I couldn't afford to go to school. My ex-partner and I had brought a house, so then we had a mortgage to worry about, just like a lot of families, and it just wasn't—it wasn't going to happen.

"It was always there, but it wasn't going to happen. Then, perfect timing, the plant I was working for closed down. That qualified all the workers to go back for job re-training, paid for by the Federal Government, thank you very much. Financing was found.

"I'd seen the ad on TV for this Program at LCC, the Chemical Dependency Counselor Program, and I thought, 'Ha!' So I found out about the application process and came over to Eugene, and picked up the application. I was nervous and freaking out, as to whether or not, they'd accept me for the Program.

"I was all scared and I was like, 'Oh my God, this is college!' In our family, it was just amazing if we graduated high school. That's all you were expected to do, get through high school.

"My sister, the one I keep referring to, my only sibling who graduated high school has gone on and has her nursing degree. She was like, 'Yea, Marty! She's been very encouraging and instrumental in my progression in pursuing this dream.

"So I filled out all the application forms and everything and sent it all in. The government paid for it, thank goodness, and here we go! I don't think I would be here if that hadn't happened, so the timing played just right for that."

I asked Marty to tell about her feelings on that first day of school.

"That first day. Oh my God! I was nervous as hell because I thought—I was thirty-three at the time I started the program and I thought . . ."

I reminded her that she'd sat next to Jan, and Jan was in her sixties.

"Yeah, It was like 'Whoo!' I was relieved. I had the old-lady jitters. I thought, 'Oh God. I'm too old to be going back and I don't like math! I don't want to do math! I hate science!'

"All that high school stuff was as if flashbacks were happening. And I was terrified because I'd been out of school for fifteen-plus years. When I was in high school, I just took what I had to take in order to get through it. I didn't take any of the—I wasn't planning on going on.

"It was scary when I first started, I really felt inferior because here were all these second-year students sitting in the classroom with us. When the instructors talked about a subject, they chimed right in. They knew what was going on and what the teachers were talking about, but things were not 'clicking' for me.

"I got more comfortable over time, made some connections with people in the Program and established some relationships. I mellowed out after the first couple of terms. Once we got settled into the routine, I was okay. It was great having that stable, one classroom all the time. That was very convenient. It was perfect for me because I need structure. I've got to have structure.

"So initially my feeing was fear and then it just felt—-when I stopped paying attention to what the other students were saying and started thinking about what the instructor was talking about, I began to understand. It was a natural thing. I don't know. I like to say it was common sense because a lot of the things they were talking about, I'd experienced with my own family.

"So there was a lot of 'Ah-ha.' That's why they did this and that's why they were having a problem. I was beginning to hear the technical terms and phrases for a lot of the things that they were doing, and at the same time, learning a lot about myself.

"I was so co-dependent. I lived with an alcoholic for a couple of years. Then it just progressed into—it just—everything seems so natural in this Program. It came naturally to me. And I've got 'it.' Whether or not, I can verbalize it is one thing, but up in my head, I've got the knowledge."

My next question for Marty was "What was the hardest part of the Program for you?"

"The counseling theories. That's what I had the most difficulty with, just because they were so dreary. Yeah, the theories thing. I couldn't handle it because it was so dry. I know it's important, but I don't know. I can't—I can't think about theories because to me, people dealing with people, isn't a theory. It's just a natural reflection.

"I'm sure I've incorporated a lot of the techniques, and if I described how I worked with people, others would say, 'Oh, that's this theory.' But I don't think about it when I'm doing it. I can't. So if you ask me now what such and such a theory is, I couldn't explain it to you. I hated that class! It was so boring! And math! I hated math! I loved pharmacology! I loved that stuff!"

I asked Marty where she wanted to be two years from now and if she was still conflicted about the direction she was going. The facility where she was counseling teens did not have the exact documentation for drug and alcohol certification. That came under a different department.

"Oh God! I hate those kinds of questions. The direction I'm going is set. It's whether or not the road is blocked, or if there's construction going on. Where I want to be and what I want to have is different. I guess it depends on how much of a sacrifice I'm willing to make. If I sacrifice where I'm working at NOW, I don't know if I'll enjoy working someplace else.

"I don't want to leave just to get that certification. Although I know that having that certification was my goal, my passion and intent was to work with addicted youth. Having certification was just one of the things that came with that.

"I'm currently working with addicted youth, but not in the capacity that we've been trained, and that we talk about in our classes. I really, really enjoy where I'm working. I don't feel comfortable walking away from there to go somewhere else and to start over—just for certification. So that's still up in the air. I'm looking at other certifications or licenses. I need to talk to some people about that.

"So right now I'm just looking forward to taking my two weeks off. Taking a two-week break after graduation, and I don't know. We'll see. Whatever happens, happens. But I didn't think I'd even get this far, and it's worked out that I have."

Marty's partner was also graduating from Lane Community College in June. She was going on to get her

Bachelor's Degree. I asked Marty if she wanted to continue with her education too.

"At this point I don't know. I feel that I've been given a lot of slack in the work that I've done. I don't necessarily feel that I've earned the grades that I've gotten. I don't feel—I think that I would be more academically challenged. I don't have enough security or self-esteem at this point to think I can handle going on to a bigger university.

"It's just such a different environment, and again, it's a fear factor. I could use the financial problems as an excuse, and right now my partner's going on for her Bachelor's and also having health problems, I keep making all these excuses. The fact is, I don't feel comfortable enough in my educational abilities to think I could handle that right now.

"And I'm just burned out. I'm burned out from school, going two-and-a half years without a break and working too. The other thing is somebody else paid for my schooling. I didn't have to pay for my LCC schooling, which was great. If that hadn't happened, I wouldn't be here. So I don't know. I won't definitely say no, but I won't say yes, either."

As soon as I asked the next question, "Where do you want to be at the end of your life?" Marty got that look in her eyes and replied "Dead." I should have known I'd get an answer like that from her especially since I'd thrown her a similar answer in one of our videos.

"I want to be dead at the end of my life, please. I don't care where I'm at as long as I'm happy."

I then asked her if there is a dream she has or something she wants to accomplish.

"No, I've never been much of a planner or dreamer. I've always been more or less an 'in the moment' person. I don't have any long-term plans. I guess that's because in our family, we didn't—that wasn't something we did. We didn't think about the future. There were no high expectations from anyone. There were no big plans. It was just work and pay the bills.

"No, I don't have any plans. As long as I'm working and paying my bills, I'm okay. Whether or not I'll still be in the same relationship, who knows? People have said before, 'This is forever' and then well—it's just not reality. So no plans."

For the last part of our interview I asked Marty if there was anything that she felt passionate about.

"I feel passionate about this field and about kids. It's a pity that we have, especially here in Lane County, such a huge problem with child abuse and meth. It's just disgusting that we, as a society, place so little value in our kids and even the adults who need help. It's just not here. There's a lot of anger and resentment toward our government and our world leaders—or, as you might call them, 'misleaders.'

"As to helping to deal with and resolve the issue, it amazes me how blind people choose to be when it comes to this. Everybody bitches and moans about it, but they won't do anything, but go on and on about politics all the time.

"I don't even think it's a money issue. They could come up with the money if they wanted to. It's just the 'want' isn't there. I think that the alcohol and drug industry is making such a profit that it goes a lot deeper than just your street dealer. It goes into politics. If somebody up there in the higher positions wasn't making any profit from this, it wouldn't be happening, and that's my 'personal' opinion. And Jan's not liable for my personal opinion."

KRISTA'S STORY

Cafeteria, Lane Community College, Eugene, Oregon, Spring 2002

Krista was twenty-nine at the time of this interview. I told her that this was not a job interview, and that our readers would want to know the problems she had in her life, how she overcame obstacles, and what keeps her going today. Since I'd been an elementary teacher, she talked to me about her son and daughter.

Krista had told me that her childhood was traumatic, and I asked her if she wanted to talk about that. Her reply was, "Where do I begin?" I asked her to discuss the events that really stood out for her.

"Oh, let's see. There's so much. It's hard to narrow down, but I guess I have my memories of my mom and her unwillingness or inability to take care of her children."

I asked Krista if her mom was an alcoholic or a drug addict.

"No, she was a 'man-aholic.' She couldn't tell men, 'No.' It didn't matter who she sacrificed in her need to pursue these men. My relationship with her is pretty distant, even to this day.

"When I was growing up, she would put on this 'look good' persona for other people, a 'model mom,' as if she were caring and loving. But behind closed doors, it was different. She was abusive, verbally abusive, and she berated me.

"I had a special-needs sister who was diagnosed with *San Filipo syndrome when she was ten. So I was probably about six or seven when that happened. We knew that she had some mental retardation, so she was already treated as the 'angel child.'

"Over the years I've built up resentment toward my mother in the relationship she had with my sister and me 'cause it was always Mom's need first. My mom's not noted for her honesty. There are so many memories that are all jumbled together, but I remember my mom and her best friend getting into an argument about my sister and me. It came out that my supposed father was not really my father and that people, whom I'd believed were just friends, were my brother and sister.

"I was pretty little. I think it all happened 'round the same time my sister was diagnosed. The house went under this major stress. My mom would admit it one day and deny it the next.

"So through my childhood and through my teen years, I was never really sure what was true, 'cause she'd change her story all the time. I wanted to believe that it wasn't true, but there is an uncanny resemblance between the brother, sister, and me. It just became clearer over the years that it was true. We have a lot of the same personality characteristics and the same physical features."

Krista confided that she had gotten herself, as so many of us did, into a big mess in her teen years. She was willing to talk about those years.

"Yeah, I was a little rebellious. Actually, I was a straight 'A' student for the first part of my teen years and the model daughter. I cared for my sister 'cause my mom got sidetracked with men and was never home. So I became my sister's caregiver. I watched her deteriorate and was angry that my life had to be put on hold for her. I'd built up pretty hostile feelings for her and would be a completely despicable person to her.

"At that time, I couldn't see that. I was a teenager. It was about me, and not about her or her illness. So I resented her, and I knew that what was going on in our house was wrong.

"Over the years I'd been speaking to government officials, but no one intervened until I took some portraits of my sister and turned them in. When they saw how emaciated she'd become in such a short time, they removed her from the home. I bailed, took off, and went here, there, and everywhere."

I asked if she had stayed with friends.

"Yeah, and people lied for me. My mom would come hunt me down—just to cause a big fight. People would hide me because they knew about our situation. That happened for a while. Then I was feeling more rebellious and had this attitude of 'I'm going to have fun. It's my turn.' I started experimenting with drugs when I was sixteen. It was a variety of this, that, and the other. I was under the influence, the first time I ever—this is embarrassing—had sex, and I got pregnant my first time.

"Can you imagine? Anyway, I lived in denial for four months saying, 'I'm not pregnant. I'm not pregnant.' And then I went to the doctor and found I was pregnant. If I had thought about any other options, they were pretty much not an option for me anymore.

"So I had my son and continued to party after I had him. Then I met up with some other people and got really wild. I started messing around with some pretty serious substances, no longer just alcohol. It was methamphetamine. I'd already had an eating disorder through my early teen years, and basically I'd found a replacement. I got involved with that for a long time.

"My son? I supported him. I just happened to have a boyfriend who supplied me with my drug of choice. I could pay my bills, but my ability to care for my child was not what it should have been. Someone could have done my son a lot of favors and intervened, but nobody did."

My next question was, "What turned you round?"

"Oh gosh! Let's see, I used for over a period of four to five years. I would say, off and on, pretty serious, and then I met my husband. My husband and I dated for about four years before we got married. He was a criminal and a drug addict, so we suited each other very well at the time.

"My husband happened to have a great police officer/detective who saw my husband as worth an effort so he was constantly in our lives. I shouldn't say his name so I'm not going to.

"I was on a very self-destructive path and this police officer—this is really hard for me to talk about—who'd been in and out of our lives turned me around.

"I was at somebody's house when they were getting busted for dealing. He came to me, told me that if I didn't get my life put together, he'd personally remove my son and daughter from me.

"Of course, I'd had people off and on tell me, 'Krista, pull it together. You know you're going to lose your children,' and I always replied, 'I don't have a problem. Blah, blah, blah. I'm having fun. I'm a good mom. I can care for my kids,' even though my life was completely not appropriate for children.

"I was living from this place to that place. There was no stable environment, no nurturing really for my children 'cause I was too preoccupied. I don't know why I didn't listen before. It was like it didn't register. For some reason, when this cop told me that he would take my kids, I believed him. I believed that he cared about my children. I guess that's why I believed he would remove them from me.

"So I went to my father-in-law's house and *detoxed, and he took care of my kids while I detoxed. I completely separated myself from the people whom I had considered my friends. My father-in-law helped me do that by telling people that I'd left, and that my husband was in jail. He made it pretty easy for me to do that. I consider him to be a father figure that I've never had before. He helped me care for and support my children. He gave me a place to live.

"It's a long time ago, though. For the most part, I forgive myself, but I still carry the guilt."

Krista mentioned that she had wanted to be a police officer. I asked if the detective's interest in her husband and her had been the reason.

"The police officer knew that I was interested. I'd discussed it with him before I applied to the Chemical Dependency Program to see if he thought that I would be a good police officer. I don't know whether he was just being nice or what, but he said, 'Yes,' and that really helped me. It was a good self-esteem thing. So I'd come to college and was going to be a great police officer. Come to find out, people who have substance use issues are not eligible to be police officers because of their potential for relapse."

I asked Krista how she decided to apply for the Chemically Dependency Program.

"I sort of fell in. I really wanted to be a police officer. When that became not possible, I was beginning to question why I was in school. What was I going to do with my life?"

I knew that Krista's husband was also enrolled at Lane Community College, so I asked her if he'd been in school at that time with her.

"Not at that time. He worked, so we could take care of our kids. So I bounced around after I found out I couldn't be a police officer. Then I was going to be a juvenile corrections officer—couldn't do that either.

"I began talking to another student in the math class about this Program. I got all excited and applied to the Program. I thought I would be denied. I actually was surprised that I was accepted. It's one of those self-esteem things. I mean, I'd already been told I couldn't be a cop, and I couldn't be a juvenile corrections officer. I wasn't a fast enough typist to be any kind of legal secretary or anything like that. So when I received the notice in the mail that I was accepted, I was grateful."

Krista agreed that ecstatic might be the word that described her elation. Then I asked her about her first day in the Program.

"Oh, my God, I was terrified. I was sitting in class, hiding in the back. On the very first day, they had some 'get to know each other' thing in Forum. I was petrified. Two of my peers latched on to me. They'd apparently known each other 'cause they were having this conversation about who was going to be my partner.

"I was scared. Right! That was—I was like this little fly on the wall. Some people back then referred to me as 'the mouse.' Me, 'the mouse?' Which you know, back then, I guess that suited me. It took me a really, long time to even get the courage to speak up in class—probably a year."

I remarked that she didn't seem to have a problem speaking up now.

"No. Sometimes. Yeah. Sometimes I have a problem, but most of the time, not. Like something'll have to get my feathers ruffled, so to speak, for me to even react."

I reminded her of how she'd had the courage to speak up about her sister. And that action showed a lot of responsibility, especially when she was so young. Then I asked her where she wanted to be two years from now.

"Oh, my God! Two years from now I'd like to be finished with my CADC 2. I would like the opportunity to have some sort of involvement with the court system. Just to better understand it, so that I can help the clients understand it."

Krista often talked about her children. I asked her if they were what kept her going.

"Most days they're my inspiration and my absolute motivation to prove that just because you mess up, that doesn't make you a bad person or worthless, or that you have no ability to make changes in your life. I think about the example I'm setting for my children, compared to the example that I set for them before, and hope that this is the one they learn the most from. Yes, yes, yes!

"Now I have five kids. Thought I should drop that in. Yeah, my son, my daughter, my stepdaughter, and two stepsons. My husband was very busy before he met me."

I asked Krista if she thought having the blended family had worked out well.

"For the most part. My husband and I've been together eleven years, and I've been involved with his kids' lives for the larger part of their lives. I'm pretty close to his daughter. I'm not as close to his middle son. I think a lot of that has to do with the relationship that I have with his biological mom. At the time my husband and I met, they'd recently separated. She was going through a difficult time, so, of course, I was the other woman.

"Right! So she's made it pretty difficult in many ways for him to have the same kind of relationship with me that I have with the other children. She was less accepting of me and passed that belief system on to him. It's been a struggle. But I think we're coming around. I think he realizes that I care about and love him. No, I'm not his biological mom, but I am and want to be considered an important part of his life."

For my last question, I asked Krista what the hardest part of the Program had been for her.

"I would say the videos. I was terrified of those. I'm harder on myself than I think most people are. I think people really are very fair to me, and so my belief system about myself is different. If someone's treating me nice, something's wrong. So I beat myself down. I'm the one who makes this Program difficult for me. If I believe everything's crisis, drama, and stressful, then I tend to do better, which is odd. But it's who I am. Yeah!"

MIKE'S STORY

Classroom, Lane Community College, Eugene, Oregon, Spring 2002

Mike was our quiet one, He didn't volunteer very often, but when he did, his observations were insightful and thoughtful. Mike also was a radio announcer for a music program on a local radio station. He was passionate about environmental issues and rode his bike to and from school.

"I'm the oldest of four, two younger brothers, and a younger sister. My childhood was rather settled, a middle class, family atmosphere, and a 'Leave it To Beaver' family. My father developed alcoholism late in my childhood. That was the first disruption of an otherwise, almost spoiled, childhood. It was easy to be a kid in that family, almost too easy.

"I'm guessing that was when I was sixteen or fifteen. I think his alcoholism became more and more severe through the years, and he flaked out. He and I, since I was the oldest, were buddies. He'd drag me out to play golf, join in with everything he was doing, and leave the other kids behind.

"His behavior got more and more irresponsible. He wasn't much a part of the family anymore. He would go on long trips or stay out late at night. He became passive, even though he was an aggressive person. His drinking made him more passive.

"Abusive? Not in any way more than stupid stuff, typical male expectations, and a bit of humiliation along with that. Nothing really abusive. He was authoritarian.

"He was pretty far gone before I started to challenge him, and eventually, I lost touch with him. I made up my mind that I didn't want anything to do with him. It took a long time before I could stand up to him. A month before his death, I had lunch with him, and we hadn't spoken for five years. So the timeliness of that was really something. I was in my mid-thirties when he had his heart attack."

We talked about Mike's schooling and early adulthood.

"I was a mediocre student who couldn't find my direction at all. In retrospect, I was into politics and sociology. I took some sociology classes at school, but was aimless with it. I didn't even declare it as a major. I hated Sacramento and didn't want to go back to the Bay Area. I dropped school, went looking for a job, and have worked ever since.

"Just some second-rate retail stuff. Eventually I had a stable, warehouse job for fifteen years, and it was so easy. I didn't have to do much of anything. I wasn't challenged at all; I went with the flow. But I also hated it, so it wasn't easy in that way. I struggled against the whole warehouse work culture. The work itself was a piece of cake and good pay."

We discussed the stress and strain of Mike's marriage.

"I was in my late twenties, and my wife was four years older. She's had some real emotional distress in her past. I call it 'Artist's Disease' because she's a brilliant artist and a really insightful person. She's the smartest person I ever met, which is ironic because she had mental illness or, at least, diagnosed mental illness.

"So now they call it 'Schizoidaffective Disorder.' That's been her latest diagnosis. But misdiagnosis remains an anomaly in the mental health area. They say she's the most uncomfortable, tortured soul they've ever met. Yet, most of the time, she's functional in getting through life. She can have great moments of joy and inspiration, but it was just too much on the marriage. So, after seven years, we became good friends.

"We came up here nine years ago as one last try for the marriage and to get her into more peaceful surroundings.

Ultimately, it's worked for her. She's been happier here and is finally making some progress. That's good to see."

Then I asked Mike what made him decide to come back to school.

"I hated my life. I wanted to follow my passion a little bit. So finally I couldn't stand it anymore, and just came down to LCC, took some career testing, combined my interests with what the college offered, and made a match.

"It's not anything inherent in the chemical dependency field. It's more the social services aspect, and I've always had a fascination with chemical dependency.

"I grew up in the 'Grateful Dead' culture of the Bay Area. I was a real 'deadhead' for a while, but completely stayed away from drugs, alcohol, and even caffeine. I've never even tried any of that except for a little bit. That gave me the fascination with chemical dependency, from the outside, looking in.

"But also, the whole sociological effects of chemical dependency and what it's doing to our society and how people are affected as individuals is intriguing to me. When I came to the career thing, I knew immediately that this is what I wanted to do."

I asked Mike if he felt close to our classmates in the Program.

"I do, not as much as I'd like, yet more than I ever thought possible. I'm a pretty reclusive person, but down deep, I don't feel that way. I want to make connections with people. I want to reach out, but for some reason, I retreat to a safety zone and don't. So part of this going back to school was challenging my comfort zone and just putting myself out there in a forced situation. I had to take Forum. I had to network. It felt so important to do that. I'm still not completely comfortable with it, but I certainly feel close to people. Graduation's going to be a big party!"

We then returned to the subject of Mike's experiences in school.

"School was something where I felt as if I were forced to be in a box. Every time I wanted to do something that I felt was creative or that people didn't quite understand, I was shoved down by the teachers and ostracized by my fellow students.

"When I was editor of the high school newspaper, the newspaper was in shambles. Whenever I came up with any ideas, it rubbed people the wrong way, and they rebelled—both my teachers and my classmates. People didn't want to revive the paper.

"I didn't find inspiration in school. It was presented as drudgery, and that's the way I took it. That's the way I behaved. School was something I had to do rather than something I could find my future with. In retrospect, I never got good counseling that would be—it would have changed my life probably. So that was frustrating. It was a series of negative consequences, but nothing that stands out as a terrible experience."

Our discussion then turned to the most influential people in Mike's life. He began speaking about his ex-wife and then about others.

"We're still best friends. I talk to her every day. I really value her and help support her. She has the house we bought together in *****. It's turned into a really good situation for her and a nice one for me to be part of from a distance. So that's why my ex-wife is still my best friend and the person I communicate with best."

Mike then turned to other people in his life who had influenced him.

"Oh, my, throughout my whole life? I guess, now that I think about it, I didn't want to be like my grandfather, my mom's father. Like my dad, he was authoritarian. Everybody loved him, but they didn't really know him. He always put on a persona. So did my dad, so I guess those two people. They were phony, and I never wanted to be like them. I hated knowing more about them than anyone else did.

"I developed an aversion to wealth, success, Republicans, and all that stuff, based around who these people were. It was a good thing for me to know them as they were because it's been a consistent pattern for me. My beliefs run counter to everything that they were all about, and I remain committed to fighting against the BS of status and privilege.

"I've had many heroes in my life. A lot of them have been political heroes and music people, even though I've never played music myself. It's who they are as people, people with whom I was fortunate enough to become friends—their integrity, their expressiveness, and the fact that they can show feeling so genuinely. Yet they have certain elements of strength. They are the people who persevere. Ruth is a great image to me of somebody who's persevered through trying times with intelligence and compassion.

"I have a friend, Keith, who's an exemplary person. He's a hero in Santa Cruz, musically, and has done it all. He helped rebuild Nicaragua when it was destroyed, and he did a bike ride up and down the entire West Coast. He's completely connected to the earth. His whole phraseology is nature-based, and he's a genuine compassionate person whose music just touches people in ways I've never seen before. He's full of magic.

"My friend, Brian, is like a god at the *Country Fair. He's the only musician who's ever been invited back to the Country Fair every year. He's not a great singer. He's not a great guitar player, but he's real, and he's such an insightful, caring person.

"So these people became heroes to me. I put them on pedestals and feel lucky to be around that energy."

We then turned to where Mike planned to be two years from now.

"I want to be educating people rather than counseling them, although I want counseling elements to come into it. I want to learn counseling more thoroughly, and realistically educate people—without being dictatorial—about tobacco and alcohol use. I'm as thoroughly disgusted with meth and cocaine even though I'm pro-legalization and against the 'Anti-Drug War.'

"I can't stand those drugs, but even more so, the legal drugs and the legal marketing of drugs. I want to be a force against the brainwashing of people. These drugs are killing them. So, in the counseling field, I've just realized how little—it's shocking how little—people know about these drugs. They deny that alcohol even is a drug. At the same time, people have a great source of knowledge where they can teach each other what they do know.

"It fascinates me—the holes that are missing in an otherwise great resource of knowledge. Somehow I'm driven to fill in those holes. So that people can put their experience, their previous knowledge, and their new knowledge together and beat this somehow.

"I don't completely know what job title I would have. I don't know if I'll go far enough to get a teaching certificate, whether it will be educating foster parents, or what form of education I'll take. I'm going to the University of Oregon to do their education, family, and human services program.

"Ultimately, I would like to do it in the schools, but somehow I'm not completely drawn to young people. I think I'd probably like working with adults more. But I feel the need to work with the younger people—junior high perhaps—because that's where decisions that they make start to take root. That's where they have to be worked with."

I asked Mike what his plans for the distant future were.

"I want to be in a place where it becomes comfortable for me to be continually learning. I want the learning process to be less painful and less something I'm fighting against. I want to be able to accept myself. It's somewhat of an 'ease into later life,' becoming good at imparting information in a realistic manner. Taking things at face value rather than clinging to my frustrations or obsessing with them.

"I want to be in social services where I work with people successfully and see ways to move and to connect with them. I want to make a real difference in people's awareness of substances and how substances affect the body and mind—so a holistic approach to how we all grow, including me."

I asked Mike if he felt that his time in the Program was a worthwhile experience.

"Yes, it's provided a foundation of learning. I've learned the ropes and come to terms with what this is all about. I can put a face on the field.

"I've gotten to know the whole range of clients and to realize that I can make huge mistakes or take the wrong approach with people. And that it's adjustable.

"It's not like out in the business world—where if you do the wrong thing, you're put down. You're dismissed, and there are threats against your job. This is more in the spirit of growth. People will come to your aid; people will give tips and pointers.

"This work really is a lifelong education process. It sets my wheels in motion and becomes empowering, knowing I'm the one who can trigger myself to look at things a bit differently. It's only then that I can make the connection with the things I've learned. It's only then that I can start to utilize them.

"I think the field is a tough one where counselors are not valued. They're sometimes invisible and only stand out when they do something wrong, or when it becomes a tough situation. Yet, I think there's so much integrity in this field and so many good people working in it, that people naturally value each other in ways that I never thought possible."

We talked about how mental health counselors and substance abuse counselors could work together.

"Mental health! Wow! It's obviously a big part of it. I think that as long as there's a respect for the client, and awareness of the other dimensions that come into it—given the lack of resources for a client—both can do their part. I think it's good for people to network and get advice from each other. But when it comes to treating a client, strengthening both fields individually seems to me a better strategy than networking with crumbs—so few resources, so little money."

My final question to Mike was if he had anything else he wished to say.

"The Program at LCC—it's been a defining moment for me in how I see the world. It's made me realize that people in recovery—the average, everyday clients, whomever they are—are all extraordinary. They're not throwaways, yet they all have this wellspring of knowledge that they can offer to each other and to the community.

"So this Program changes the definition of how people are valued as human beings. It empowers people by osmosis, by just being there, and by being a good solid Program. It helps people to do the redefinition rather than leading them by the nose.

"I'm grateful that you're doing this—exposing what this is all about because we have to learn from a new definition of learning itself—learning about learning. There's a term for that—epistemology. This Program has shown that we don't have a clue how to learn.

"Education is a buzzword, but we don't know what it means. This Program has redefined for me what education is and how education can be transformational in ways that go beyond the lifetime of some people's education.

"This is true learning for me, and it's going to be lifelong. I'm really grateful that somehow I got sucked up in it. I'm still not quite sure how that happened, but I feel really lucky."

DAWN'S STORY

Classroom, Lane Community College, Eugene, Oregon, Spring 2002

Dawn joined us the spring of our first year. She was very quiet during that term. By the second year, she'd become a valued person in our class.

My first question was about her childhood.

"There were many important things. I was left on an orphanage doorstep and adopted through an agency. My foster parents brought me to Germany because the father was a teacher there. They didn't treat me right, so another family intervened. At two-and-a-half, I was adopted by this couple that I refer to as my mother and father.

"My mother was German-American and my father was Jewish. So, at two-and-a-half, I learned how to walk, talk, and all that other good stuff. I guess that the significance of that for me has been being challenged because I got a late start. I didn't know how to really talk until I was two because nobody ever talked to me up until that time. Then I lived in Germany until I was eight and moved to Eugene.

"I grew up in Eugene, went to college in Portland, studying pre-med, psychology, and natural science while I was looking into the medical field. I'd been brought up with a different view on people, medicine, and health, and I didn't quite like or agree with the American medical perspective. I decided before investing another hundred thousand in medical school, I should take a step back and really examine what I wanted to do."

I knew Dawn was not in recovery, but I asked her about friends or family with addiction problems.

"Yeah, you know, I've been pretty dense about the whole thing. To be perfectly honest, even though I always heard in school about kids using drugs, I never saw it. I wouldn't even know if anyone was using even if it was right in front of me.

"I was involved with someone who drinks too much and definitely has an addiction problem. My last partner also was an alcoholic, and this is part of how I came into this field. One of my friends asked me if I knew anything abut addiction and I said, 'No, I don't.' She said that I should probably find out about it, and that might help clarify some of the difficulties I was having.

"I lived in San Francisco for a while, and I came back because I'd been taking care of my grandparents. They'd gotten into a car accident. So I came back to Eugene in 1996 to care for my grandmother, who had Alzheimer's, until she passed away. I worked for a marketing company. The company closed, and I was back home taking care of my grandfather. I was bored at home so I took 'Understanding Addictive Behavior,' which was an evening class."

I asked her who her instructor had been and she replied, "Jessica." Jessica was also our Forum coordinator.

"It actually was very good that she was my instructor because I think—I guess it was a lot of work. I didn't really think it was. I thought it was a lot less work than I had been accustomed to. I thought we got off easy by getting a study guide because I remember that in college I had to review five hundred pages and yet had no idea what was going to be on the exam.

"So I thought I got off easy, and I really, really appreciated her teaching because she challenged me. It was fast-paced, and it—she complemented my style of learning. And I picked up the counseling class. She was also teaching that. That's what intrigued me about this Program."

We talked a little bit about how quiet she had been when she first joined us in the class about drugs. Neither of us could remember exactly when we first met.

"You know, I felt like an 'out' person. Everyone knew each other, and I didn't know anybody."

I asked Dawn if she still felt that way.

"No! No! No! I think it was in 'Group Therapy' class that I decided that I wasn't an 'out' person and that I could probably join the group. I've been thinking about what I want to do, about going back to med school, and the work that will be involved in applying to med school. I'm not really sure if I'm ready to tackle it.

"I'm interested in psychology and want to help other people. This Program piqued my interest because I know that drug and alcohol misuse affects many, many people, and would be a good base for me to have. Even if I were to move onto other areas in medicine or in psychology, this would be a great foundation for me to have.

"There are a lot of myths about addiction. Even to this day, I'm still working through some of them. Looking back, I can see where the addictions process was interplaying with my relationships. At the time, I had no idea, and now I have more of a framework in which to put it."

I asked Dawn how old she was and where she planned to be in two years.

"I'm thirty-four. Two years from now? That's a good question. I'd like to have experience. I don't know what group therapy really looks like. I've never been through it, haven't been exposed to it. I'd like to be able to have clarified my interests more. I might be starting another Master's or Ph.D. program in a couple of years."

Then I inquired about where she saw herself in five years.

"Five years from now, what I'd like is to find a niche where I'm really satisfied with my work. What I envision for myself is eventually moving into consulting or being able to offer it within this community. When I say this community, I also mean the surrounding areas.

"I'll probably stay in Oregon, for sure. But I'm feeling flexible. Right now, I'm tied to Eugene because of my grandfather, but once he passes on, then there's nothing that's really tying me to this area. But I'd like to find some kind of niche where there's a need that's not being filled and developing something. I have no idea what that is at the moment."

We talked about her vision and plans for her entire life.

"I've held a vision since I was ten. My primary goal is more of a process then an ending. It's more about being able to fulfill my potential. That involves, obviously, my work, becoming a person, gaining confidence, being able to blossom, and to contribute in ways that I want to.

"The vision that I've had for a long time is one where I'm not just in survival-mode, but also doing all right financially. I've come to determine that's very important for me. I need to be financially okay. And I think that there are ways that I can do this kind of work and also have that kind of prosperity, without them being in conflict with each other.

"The other thing is I've always imagined developing an organization, or being in support of an 'organization.' This is a vision I've had, and I've no idea if this is going to be realized or not. I want to work with an organization where business people take care of the financial aspect, and the counselors and the people, who are really good at what they're doing, can do the service part. I want to structure it so that there are people good at self-care involved. And there's enough support from the management for the workers, so that everyone can maintain their mental health and receive organizational help.

"I think it's really important to have an organization that's healthy because that's what we're promoting, or what we're selling. What we are offering is health—within the drug and alcohol field. One really important aspect of that is modeling correct behavior. To accomplish that, you need an organization that models correct behavior.

"I think I'm pretty pragmatic in my vision. My first step is actually becoming familiar with an area, instead of saying, 'Oh yeah. I can do all these things,' even when I have no idea what it looks like. One thing I can offer is that I'll stay open to experiences and opportunities. And as they present themselves, I'll take advantage of them. So if I find an opportunity where I can develop something that creates or helps an organization become healthy, stay healthy, and function healthily, sure, I'll go for it. Absolutely!"

Dawn then discussed the hardest part of the Program for her, other people, and events that had a major influence in her life.

"I would say there are several things. One is just the self-growth process because there are a lot of things that stimulated me. The other thing that I think is really challenging is breaking though my own denial of what addiction looks like.

"While I haven't had drug or alcohol addiction myself, I understand what addiction is and I've probably—if I really think about it—had other addictions. I've spent so much time in relationships with people who have been active in their addiction. I've enabled them and was very active in the denial aspect of it. One of my challenges is to break though the denial to where I can recognize signs, symptoms, and denial without enabling.

"Yeah, I'm pretty good at denial. Let's see what else? I've always thought of myself as being extremely fortunate where my life has gone. There's been a lot of experiences that have definitely created character for me or given me opportunity to create character for myself.

"One of them was moving to the United States with my mother, a friend of hers, and my maternal grandparents. Two years later, when I was ten, my mother passed away from cancer. I was fortunate that all the adults in my life asked me what I wanted. I didn't want to move. I didn't want anything to change. So her friend became my guardian, but she passed away when I was fifteen. I took care of her for two years while she was dying of cancer.

"Then I knew someone who had a tremendous impact on me. When I was in the ninth grade, this person committed suicide five blocks from my house. That affected me for a long time afterwards.

"I also had a friend murdered by her sister's boyfriend. He murdered my friend and her father. My friend, the victim, had to work with them, and she always presented a very happy-go-lucky, smiling face to everyone. I finally broke into that shell, the day before she was killed. I had talked to her and asked how it was going. She was worried about her sister, and we said we'd talk about it on Monday because it was going into the weekend.

"That was the first time she actually opened up, at least to me, and let down her guard. She didn't come to school on Monday, and I found out she was killed. Some other kids I knew committed suicide, so there's been a lot of death trauma."

Dawn talked about how she learned to recognize herself as an enabler and learned to set boundaries.

"I think one of the challenges has also been thinking about boundaries because I've been an enabler, wanting to rescue. I think that being on that triangle was very useful.

"Last summer I had an incident with a woman. She and I had become friends. She was interested in more than that. She was rather delusional about the whole thing. I couldn't understand. I kept setting boundaries, and she kept trying to push beyond them. And then what I'd hear from other people about what she said was very different from my reality with her.

"We had a phone call that was pretty traumatic for me because I was doing suicide intervention—or at least I thought I was. I'd done it with friends before. I was on the phone with her for two-and-a-half-hours, trying to do the suicide intervention. I kept hearing a gun clicking in the background, and it was really, really intense.

"Any time I wanted to get off the phone, I'd hear the gun click. Oh, my God! I didn't want to hang up and didn't remember her address. I called her friend and had her friend go over there, but she wouldn't let the friend inside. I wanted to call the police. But her friend said, 'Don't have the police come over because she has a gun, and that's not a good idea.'

"And then it was four in the morning. I finally said, 'Well, you know I'm really tired. I don't know what you need, and I have a job interview in the morning.' Then, just like that, her voice changed and she said, 'Oh, my God, if I'd known you had a job interview, I would never have called.'

"Just that sense of ultimate betrayal was difficult. It was good that I went through that because I understand a lot more now about boundaries and rescuing, about what's appropriate, and what happens when I don't set boundaries. Not only what happens for me, but what happens for the other person. Had I not listened to her friend and called the police, she might have gotten the intervention that she needed."

I asked Dawn if they were still friends.

"No, no! I really had to cut it off because every time I talked to her, she would reengage in the same ways she did before, and that triggered something in me. This wasn't working for me at all. I had that sense of being so drained emotionally. The vision I had was of feeling like gravel. The riverbed is dry and it's all gravel. Then I know that I'm done and realize that I can't get to that state, especially in this work."

For my final question I asked Dawn if she had anything else she wanted to say about the Program or her life.

"I think this Program's great. I'm sad about leaving. I think the information that I've gained is important. On one hand, I think everybody has this information, and it seems pretty common sense. On the other hand, I realize that I didn't know any of it when I walked though the door the first time. And how crucial—Ruth always talked about having a paradigm shift or reframing—it is to really understand the addictive process in order to actually be of help. I know the myth of denial and the social pressures for denial. All that stuff touches pretty much everybody. I know that a difference can be made, and education is a key element to that."

CARSTEN'S STORY

Classroom, Lane Community College, Eugene, Oregon, Spring 2002

Carsten returned to the Chemical Dependency Counseling Program after a year off to work in retail. He joked a bit before he talked about his history of addiction and recovery. I asked him if there were some things he'd rather not remember.

"I've come to terms with most of it, so I'm not too worried about that. I guess I did a lot of stuff where I punched my family out of my life to the point that when I actually did get into recovery, I didn't feel that I had a family.

"Family of origin? Mother, sister, grandmother, and I pushed them away. At the time I thought they were just nuts. So there's a lot of distancing myself from the family. It started out with arguments. Then I went to stealing. I don't know why, but they kept cash in their dresser drawers. Once I found that, it was all over.

"I think that was when I was eleven. I've been trying to figure that out lately. My father died when I was eleven in April 1993. I was in the sixth grade.

"If you go back into my childhood, I was the kid who got sips of beer from his dad and never thought much about it. Then there was a liquor cabinet that didn't have a ton of liquor. My parents, my mother especially, were not heavy drinkers. My dad was very controlled about it.

"He'd made a decision when they got married to change his life, and so he and my mother did. They partied with friends and would make grasshoppers with crème de menthe and ice cream, but it wasn't anything major. The same bottle of vodka must have been in that cabinet for years."

We discussed what made Carsten eliminate alcohol from his life.

"How lonely it got. How pathetic I got. Lately I've been remembering because I share my story with lots of people. Right near the end, I was in Missoula, Montana; I had been out at the bars for quite a while, typical behavior for me. I was into gambling too—that's another part of it. I remember coming out of this bar and walking down the sidewalk. I thought for sure that I was walking a straight-line because I was so controlled over how I was acting.

"I was trying my hardest to look sober, and a guy, across the street with a group of people, was pointing, laughing, and making fun of me. So I walked across the street, calling him on. I'm really not the violent type but here I was trying to pick a fight with this guy because he was making fun of me. I remember that I only came up to his chest, so I'm glad nothing came of it.

"The one thing that he said that I still remember today, as if I were sober at that moment, was 'Just go home. You're pathetic!' It just whooped into my heart. It wasn't too long after that moment that I actually got sober."

Carsten then discussed his experience with Alcoholics Anonymous.

"I went to A.A., and I can't explain it. I knew A.A. was there, but I don't remember ever hearing about it. It's possible that I did, in health class or something. I called them. I'd actually called them once before, but they couldn't provide what I needed, which was a meeting where I could walk in and not be recognized by anybody. It also had to be non-smoking!

"It had to be non-smoking because I couldn't stand cigarette smoke. Even though I use nicotine, I don't smoke. I chew, but I can't stand cigarette smoke. They couldn't do that. Then I got bad enough that I didn't care if it were non-smoking, or if people recognized me."

Carsten explained that he went to his first A.A. meeting on September 18, 1994, when he was about twenty-three, and he's now thirty.

"You know, it's weird. I was scared, like anybody would be. I was going into a place where I was the outsider. At least that's what I thought, but I was amazed.

"I went in, and the whole meeting was about me. I don't see it as much here, but in Montana whenever somebody comes in for their first meeting or if they've had a relapse, the topic usually is the *first step in the *twelve steps. I didn't know it at the time, but they were having a first-step meeting. Everyone who shared talked directly to me.

"At first I was really uncomfortable, but after awhile, I started listening and heard some stuff. There were a couple of things that I took away from that first meeting that I still hold with me today.

"After the meeting, everyone was leaning me over the literature counter that they had, just being nice. I say 'leaning me over,' because they were as close to me physically as anyone had been in a while. I was real uncomfortable with that, but I knew I needed to get sober. I think that's what kept me going back. Part of it was also intimidating, but it was what I needed. I knew that I needed to stay sober!"

I asked Carsten if he'd liked school and if he knew why or why not.

"I hated school! To be honest with you, I think it was because I wanted to do what I wanted to do. They had structure. I had to be a certain place at a certain time. I found that I broke rules just to break rules. Not with any message that I was trying to send except for, 'I'm me, and I'm going to do whatever the hell I want.' It didn't matter what they wanted."

Carsten then commented on his "close" relationship with the principal.

"I'd say we were on a first name basis, but that was because I called him by his first name just to piss him off. His name was Dick so it made it really interesting to say, 'How ya doin, Dick?' with a whole bunch of meaning behind it.

"I actually liked quite a few of my teachers. I've always been told that I'm very bright and, in looking back, maybe it was boredom. I never really tried to get into the honors classes. I never wanted to be a 'brainiac,' so I actually worked my way into survey English—the lowest English that you could take in high school.

"There I was. I knew the English language and how to write and everything. I was a good writer, but because of my grades and not putting anything into it, they had to put me in that class. And so I ended up in this class with all the 'stoners,' and it was wonderful. I mean I was expected to do the work, but the work was so easy. It wasn't a challenge at all.

"Then I worked my way back into regular English. When I finally made a decision to go to college, I was going to major in English because I loved reading stories, and I wanted to write. I was also going to do the secondary education part, so I could teach. I was going to do the English as a double major. It was really weird."

Carsten discussed what attracted him to the Chemically Dependent Counselor Training Program.

"Because I was a recreation student at the University of Montana and in recovery, I got this outstanding opportunity with a great group of people, and through that I did a lot of volunteer stuff. So, out of that, I did a presentation on recovery from addiction. I could see that programs like Outward Bound and the National Outdoor Leadership in Knowles, Montana, see a lot of people who're having trouble in their lives and want change. They think that nature will bring that on. I did a presentation about that, and one of the instructors slyly handed out this thing about the Wilderness Treatment Center in Marion, Montana.

"I went there as an intern-guide for the treatment center. They use these wilderness trips as part of the curriculum, and I fell in love with this program. I fell in love with the staff. A counselor who was on that first trip is now the director. He and I are friends of sorts, and that's where I'm going to work when I'm done with this.

"It's dandy treatment for males, fourteen through twenty-four. Their program is set up, so that they have thirty days of inpatient treatment—standard, traditional treatment. Then they go anywhere from a sixteen- to-twenty-one day wilderness trip, dependent upon the season. In the winter, it's shorter.

"Then they come back and have a week where they prepare for aftercare, and typically they're moved to a halfway house somewhere else in the nation. They actually send kids all over the place."

Carsten discussed the trauma of his dad's death and how it affected him.

"It's still probably the worst thing that's happened to me. I think that's where my road started as far as addiction is concerned. And I'm really grateful for this Program—to recognize some of the things that happened to me and to attend the classes.

"I think about it quite a bit, especially in the 'Youth Addiction' class and the trauma that happens. Now we're in 'Gender Issues,' and I'm seeing more. If you look at my family tree, every male in my family is already dead. I'm the only one left. I'm the last one with this last name too."

Carsten discussed trying to reengage with his family and talked about how his father's death alienated him from his family and his church.

"I'm getting closer with my family as the years go by. It's a process of getting back together. I think it just shocked the hell out of me that my dad was gone. Everything was shaking. At that point, the preacher's wife hugged me and said, 'Sometimes God's will is hard to understand,' something to that effect, or maybe, 'This is just God's will.'

"Up until I was eleven, I'd been a pretty devout Christian. That's all I knew, and I enjoyed the church, my family, other families, kids that I hung out with, and the good times that we had. It was a lot of fun. I didn't necessarily enjoy the church service because it's boring for a kid, but the community around that was great.

"So when my dad died and she said that, I remember thinking, 'Well then, F*** God.' He just took everything. I really loved my dad. We had a great relationship together. So when that happened, my religion and belief system were completely shaken, and I just went with it."

Then we went on to Carsten's feelings and thoughts about spirituality.

"Spirituality is the basis of my recovery in that A.A. is where I got sober. It's gotten a lot simpler than when I was a kid. Just a 'There is a God, and I'm not it.' I've come to believe that. And I've gone through the gamut. I looked at Native American theology and their spirituality. I've looked at Buddhism. I've taken classes on Christianity and the Bible in college to try to understand both better.

"And throughout all of it, I think it just comes down to a kind of melting pot. I've taken little bits and pieces of each. One of my core beliefs is that this life is a classroom, and we get to come back and do it over.

"Maybe there's a little time off. Then we come back and try to learn the next set of spiritual truths, or we move on to the next plane that can give us those lessons.

"My wife and I use spirituality in our relationship. We draw things on a triangle, the line between her and me, between her and God, and between God and me. We try to live our lives as close to that as we can. Of course, we fall off every once in a while."

Carsten then related the story of how he met his wife.

"I met her in recovery. She's in recovery too. I actually met her mom first. Her mom and I were in this class at the University of Montana, and I remember walking out of class and saying to her, 'You're the lady from A.A.,' because she was a pretty outspoken member of that group. So we started talking. I'd met my wife already, but I didn't know they were mother and daughter. So her mom credits the whole thing to that and says that we're together because of her, but it's not quite that way.

"My wife and I met first. Then I found out that they were mother and daughter. It was interesting. I guess that's part of that spirituality too. I think it was just set up that way. I have no doubt that I'm doing what I'm supposed to be doing right now. I didn't have that for a long time, so—in our relationship—I don't doubt at all.

"My wife's working with children with severe emotional disturbances. She's an outreach worker and treatment specialist. I forget the title. Then she's also playing with the kids a little bit and has family meetings."

We then talked about Carsten's plan for two years from now.

"I want to be at the Wilderness Treatment Center in Montana, doing the deal, and hopefully in our own house."

We progressed to Carsten's plans for five years from now. He thought about it before he answered.

"I'd like to still be at the Wilderness Treatment Center. I think this is a long-term thing. I'd hope to be in a less intense role by that point because the wilderness trips take a toll.

"Hopefully then, and I'm scared about this, maybe a family will be happening. If we have kids, it will be rough to leave my wife for three weeks. It will put a lot of strain on her. So I don't know, probably a less intense role."

I asked him where he'd like to be at the end of his life.

"In Montana—fly fishing."

Carsten voiced his homesickness for Montana.

"I haven't got the great connection here in Eugene that I do back home in Montana. I go to A.A. meetings when I'm back there and see old friends. My *sponsor's back there. I talk to him once a week.

"I never clicked with Eugene, the town itself, and I don't know why that is. In the suicide class, our instructor talked about the fact that Eugene has a silent elitism about it. He was putting words to what I've thought during the three years that I've been here.

"In Montana, if I go into a gas station to pay for my gas, there's a chance I might have a ten-minute conversation behind the counter, and here, I just don't get that. People don't say, 'Hi,' to me on the street.

"In fact, a big complaint of mine has been that when I'm driving up to the forest, on my way fishing, nobody waves back at me. In Montana, we always wave to each other. So I've really missed that human connection. It's just not been here for me. I'm definitely 'chompin at the bit' to get out of here."

I asked Carsten what the hardest thing in the Program was for him.

"I think the hardest thing in the Program was to get my mind to open up. I had definite ideas about what recovery was, what treatment should be, and how people should be treated. As I've gone along, I've made a definite shift in thinking—a lot more open-mindedness, a lot less directional attitude, or 'in your face' type stuff.

"I still believe that counselors should be directive. I don't buy into *Carl Roger's thinking, 'Let the client determine the direction of the counseling.' because even when I was sober enough, I still needed direction. I needed somebody to say, 'Okay, here is A, you do A. Then we'll do B, and then we'll do C.' It made things so much easier for me, just as in life."

Carsten also indicated that he might like teaching.

"At the college level, maybe. I must be moving onto the next level, which could be teaching, consulting, or even having a private counseling practice. I don't know. I just don't know.

"I'm pretty close to a Bachelor's Degree with the schooling that I already have, so I'd like to finish that and do a Master's. The thought's crossed my mind, but that's a long ways away."

For my final question, I asked Carsten if he had anything he wanted to add about anything we'd been discussing.

"I don't think the wilderness programs are given the attention that they should be given. I've also worked at another program, which is just traditional, inpatient treatment, and it was so damm clinical and so sterile that I felt uncomfortable.

"We don't hear a lot about wilderness programs in this Program. I think it'd be nice to see more of that around because of the kids that I see come through.

"It's amazing what happens to them out there. The wilderness actually teaches them quite a bit. I think it gets them in touch. It's weird. It jerks kids back into line, into practicality, and a pragmatic way of thinking, 'Well if I don't cook my food, I'm not going to eat.'

"The whole point with WTC is that they're very focused. They'll tell somebody, 'You know, you're probably not a client who can benefit from us because we're going to talk about addiction and only addiction.' Obviously there's some give-and-take.

"What I see happening in the nonprofit or more public institutions is they're trying to be everything to everybody. My questions have always been, 'Why don't you try to be a good addiction treatment center? Why don't you try to be a good mental health treatment center?' Then we'll work collaboratively together instead of 'Why don't we stretch our budget even thinner and add another program?' It doesn't make sense to me."

DEBORAH'S STORY

Classroom, Lane Community College, Eugene, Oregon, Spring 2002

When we first knew Deborah, she was very quiet, but always had a big smile. She was short with blond hair. One morning she came to school with her hair in a modified spike, and we all loved it. We began to see the mischievous side of Deborah's personality. She was a good friend to everyone.

The first subject of our interview was Deborah's childhood.

"My childhood was pretty good. I remember it clear back until I was two years old. I suffered a lot from ear infections and was in pain a lot. My grandmother ran a daycare for kids, and I spent a lot of time there with all the kids. It was like a school. My favorite time was 'sit-and-story' time. My grandmother would tell stories. We had little dolls that we'd dress up, and she'd tell us stories about different cultures. It was a happy time except when I was sick.

"My dad worked at Fort Stevens [near Astoria, Oregon], and my mom was home. I can remember her being pregnant with my little sister.

"Then we moved away. We left my grandma and the daycare center. That was pretty traumatic for me. I went through a separation type thing where I was rebellious and hated everything because we had to move.

"I was four. Then we moved out to the farm where I live now. My grandma joined us, and it was much better when she was living there."

I knew Deborah was not in recovery, but I asked her how alcohol has affected her life.

"My dad's sister died ultimately from alcoholism. She and my uncle were always drunk when we visited their house every other weekend. They had kids, and their house was always a mess. I remember walking into the house and seeing their distillery back in the kitchen. They made their own beer and wine.

"After I got older, I realized what they were doing. My uncle developed diabetes and finally had both his legs cut off. He's quit drinking, and his family is taking care of him because he can't get around by himself.

"My aunt finally got sent to a residential treatment center, and just lost it—alcoholic dementia. The last time I remember her, she was like a child. She would make things like a little kid would—bows in her hair She's somewhat happy, but still her mind's gone. That's really sad."

We talked about Deborah's first marriage and her children.

"My daughter's thirty-one, and my son's twenty-four. I got married when I was seventeen. My first husband drank a lot and was quite abusive when he was drunk.

"I was married to him for eleven years. A lot of the time, he wasn't home because he was a truck driver. So he was gone a lot, and he'd send just enough money to pay the bills. I went to work because I needed extra things like clothes for the kids and me. I needed to be out, making my own way, so I separated myself that way.

"Then he got a local job. He'd met someone up north. He was messing around as usual. I guess he did it the whole time we were married.

"We were having problems, and I saw him at our friends' house. He'd been gone for two days, I told him that if he didn't come home, he'd find his things in the yard, and that was it. I was working and felt that he'd totally destroyed everything. So I called him a name because he said that if anyone was leaving this time, it was me, and he was keeping the kids. The old Mother Bear in me came out, and I called him a really foul name.

"I'm not used to cussing, but, boy, I did, and he jumped up and started beating me. His friend wouldn't stop it. The friend's wife, who was only four-foot-eleven and weighed about ninety-eight pounds, jumped on his back. He just brushed her off.

"He'd hit me. I'd fall down, and he'd kick me until I got up. I always got up! That's one thing! I can't stay down! I'll get up until I'm unconscious. I was black all down the left side and had boot marks on me. I went into the hospital for three days. When I got out, I picked up a do-it-yourself, divorce kit, took my kids to my parents, and divorced him."

We digressed a bit to talk about how Deborah supported herself and the friend who helped her.

"I worked in a Chinese restaurant. It was a lot of fun. I worked there for seven years. They just took me in, protected me, and treated me like I was part of the family. It was a very healing experience for me. In those days, in the middle and late seventies, you could survive on those wages. I supported two kids and myself on wages and tips. You didn't have to report your tips back then.

"My best friend drove me to the Chinese restaurant to get the job. She and I did a lot of partying back then. She definitely had a problem with alcohol and all other kinds of drugs. And she's been my friend for thirty years. I've seen her go through a lot of hard times, and she's been clean and sober for fourteen years. She's had a lot of influence on me."

We returned to Deborah's other marriages and relationships.

"Since my first marriage, I've been in other relationships. One relationship I had was with an alcoholic. When he started sobering up after we got together, we found out he was schizophrenic. He was covering up his symptoms that way. Our relationship ended because of his problems and of my problems.

"Then I was in a relationship with another man who was a special-ed teacher. He was black and a wonderful man. My kids loved him, my parents loved him, and I loved him. He was also an alcoholic. We were together over a year when his drinking just got to be too much. He wasn't even considering recovery. That ended, and I did a lot of moving around.

"I got into another relationship and married a man in the military and was with him for seven years. I raised his two boys. The younger boy has schizophrenia. We found that out when he was entering puberty. His dad totally refused to see it. Then the boy started using substances, covering it up when he became a teenager.

"I couldn't help him. We were overseas, and the military authorities wouldn't do anything unless the *sponsor, my husband, asked for help. My husband refused to ask for help for his son. My son lived with us then. My daughter was grown-up and getting married at that time.

"My husband wasn't much of a drinker, thank goodness. I think that's probably one reason I married him. I felt that that might be secure, and I fell in love with his kids and raised them. When they were gone, and my stepson finally went off the deep-end and took off, I took my son and left too. I came back to Oregon. I stayed with my mom and my grandma and started taking care of them. Then I got into nursing home work."

I knew Deborah really liked her nursing home job, and I asked her to tell me about that.

"I really do like it—especially where I work now with Alzheimer's and other dementia patients. I've dealt with a lot of people who have alcoholic dementia and live in our place. I worked with their families It's such a devastating thing and so preventable.

"While I was working there, we had lots of people enrolled at a chemical dependency center who volunteered where I work. That's how I got to know other addicts besides my friend—the one who called me in her deepest addiction and called me even when I was overseas.

"I got to know those addicts and alcoholics who came to work and volunteer with us. They were so caring and compassionate. They seemed even more sensitive then other people I know. I felt that I wanted to help. If there had been some kind of early intervention, life would have been better for them."

I asked Deborah how she decided to apply for our Program.

"I met my present husband, a recovering alcoholic, who runs recovery houses. A friend of his was graduating from this Program. I learned a little about it from her. I thought it was great and something I felt strongly that I wanted to do. So I gave it a try."

I asked Deborah how she felt on our first day of class.

"Excited! I had doubts about me—somebody who had not been in recovery being able to help. But my friend, who works at the relief nursery, told me that some of the best counselors she knows haven't been in recovery."

I knew that Deborah had a lot of decisions to make and asked her about that.

"I'm soul-searching about getting my degree and my CADC 1. I've been trying to wean myself away from the Alzheimer's facility where I work. It's really hard. I love those people. Part of the reason I decided to do something different is because it hurts so much when they die. I've sat with probably two hundred people as they passed away. Sometimes their families weren't able to get there in time. I realize that the dying isn't the hard part for my patients, it's the having to live the way they do.

"It's so hard on them and so hard on the families too. It's such an extended grief: years and years of it. It's similar to the grief that families of people with addiction suffer. Their loved ones seem to be getting better, but then they relapse. They get better and relapse again.

"Families have recently come to me and told me how much it mattered to them for me to be there. My boss, although she's been very supportive of my going to school, has begged me to take on more work. They've had some people in transition who've come in and tried—it just doesn't work for them.

"They trust me to do all aspects of the job: the paperwork, dealing with families, and there's nobody better at doing what I do for them. There are probably people who are just as good, but I'm feeling a lot of responsibility to be there. I'm torn. Summer's coming and I've agreed to take on a lot more work then.

"I started CO-OP this term, but so much has been going on in my life. My mom passed away in March, and I got married in December. It's just been too much. I've picked up an extra day at work, and in the summer, I'll probably start working five days. I still have CO-OP and math to finish. I'm still trying to decide whether to go and get my CADC 1.

"I'll have the summer to think about it. I'm not going to decide everything right now. All my schooling that I've had up until now hasn't been wasted at all because it's helped me at work.

"We have several girls with us who are recovering, and some are on the work release from jail. And, gosh, they're wonderful girls. We've had several successes. I've been able to interact with them so much better and with so much more understanding than I could have before I took this Program."

I asked Deborah if she had plans for five years from now.

"Five years from now? I expect I'll be having my own little farm with my husband. I'd originally planned on working at the recovery houses with my husband, and I still might.

"Right now, my husband and I don't live together. Part of my time problem is working, going to school, and having enough time for my husband. Not to mention my kids, my grandkids, and my brother and sister who have been having a really rough time since my mom passed way. They need my support too. So that's why I decided to simplify for now, give up the CO-OP, and work. But at work, it doesn't really seem like work because I have so much fun when I'm there."

I asked Deborah where she hoped to be and what else she wanted to accomplish in her life.

"I would like to leave people happy. I would like to have accomplished helping people feel better. See my grandchildren with productive lives, not with huge financial success, but content with their lives and happy being alive."

For my last question I asked Deborah what the hardest thing in the Program was for her.

"The hardest thing? Seeing people come and go. I haven't been able to keep in contact with a lot of people who have been in the Program. I've learned so much from people in my first year. There were people, who graduated last year, who really taught me a lot by their actions.

"I love to see the way people grow. I think that they don't get it, and all of a sudden, I see little lights dawning in their eyes. It's just amazing.

"As far as all the learning, it was really hard, but it was so exciting. Learning about yourself is difficult, and there are a lot of things I found out about myself."

MARIE'S STORY

Patio, Oakway Center, Eugene, Oregon, Summer 2002

At twenty in the fall of our first year, Marie was our youngest class member. She didn't talk a lot, and she was in the other Forum group. So I didn't get to know her well that first year. We talked more the second year, and after this interview, I was sorry that we hadn't become better acquainted during our two years in the Chemical Dependency Program.

My first question to Marie was about her childhood.

"I grew up in *****. Both of my parents are addicts, so I was raised in the drug world. I went through a period with drinking and smoking pot. I remember drinking because it was so accepted in the family. I started smoking pot when I was fourteen."

I asked Marie if growing up in that environment contributed to her involvement in drugs and alcohol.

"It did. It did because my parents mainly used crank, and I was the goody-two-shoes of the family. So when I started smoking pot, I fit in more with my family. That was something we could do together—sit around and get stoned."

Marie talked about her school years. She didn't like school.

"In my teen years, I didn't want to be anywhere. I didn't want to be at school. I didn't want to be at home. I just wanted to run around with my friends. I moved in-and-out between my mom, my dad, my aunts, and some friends of the family. I just moved around."

Marie explained what changed her.

"I didn't want to be like my parents. I didn't want to have the life that they had. When I was a teenager, I was really depressed and wondering, 'Why did I get the bum deal?' One day I was lying in bed crying, and I thought, 'Why is this a bum deal? This could be my opportunity.' So I decided that I'd help other people and families who've experienced the same kind of things.

"I've gone to A.A. meetings on and off over the years and I used go to *N.A. with my mom when she had to, but that was for her, not for me."

We talked about her impression of the first day and the Program in general.

"Right out of high school, I decided I wanted to do college. And that lasted like a week. On the first day of this Program, I was terrified. I was only twenty, and everybody in the room was older than me. The first part is just a blur to me. It was all about surviving, getting into it.

"The hardest part of the Program was looking at myself, so it's a lot of self-evaluation, and that's never really easy. I kept up with the material just fine. I don't think I remember it all right now, but it's somewhere in my head. That was a lot of cramming. I liked everything pretty much, but I didn't like the paperwork classes—learning how to do case management."

We talked about Marie's employment and where she might do her internship.

"I've been there for five years. I like my boss and my co-workers. The job I can live without.

"I did an interview a couple weeks ago at an adult center, but I really want to do just teens. I don't want to do adults. I worked at ***** for a while. It lacked the structure I need."

I asked her if she'd talked to a classmate of ours who worked at a facility for teens.

"I'm going to check into that, and I'm going to check into *****. They have a small teen program. My dad is in one program at *****, so I don't want to go there."

We talked about her siblings. Her face lit up when she talked about her brother who is four.

"I don't get to baby-sit him a lot because of my schedule, but when we get to hang out for the day, it's so fun. He's smart. He's very smart. If I go further with my education, it's going to be in a different field. I'm actually discovering that I really like little kids.

"One of my brothers is going be a father in a couple of months—a niece. The other one turned eighteen yesterday in *****. He'll be put in an adult lockup in a few months. He's spent every birthday since he was fourteen in one lock-up facility or another, so he doesn't have a good track record."

We then discussed the cancellation of our Program at LCC, and how she felt about that and our classmates.

"I don't know. I know that part of me is relieved because I made it. And another part of me is disgusted with money, with politics. It's all politics, but they don't realize it. They don't care about the effects on everyday people.

"I enjoy all of my classmates, even the ones that most people didn't care for. What I really love about our group is how it's so diverse, and how we all have our own reasons for being there. But we all believe in the same cause. Even what's his name? He believed in the cause and stuck it out that first year, and no matter how many people disagreed with his opinion, he still offered it.

"It was a really intense two years to be spending with the same people. Writing so much about each other—that's intense and a long time to hang out with each other. Sometimes you've heard the same stories so many times from certain people, but that's their story. They're not done with it yet.

"Unfortunately, I didn't get very close to anyone. I think a big part of it was my fear about my age. I was trying to join in conversations when people were talking about their spouses, their kids, and other stuff. I don't have any of that."

We talked about where she hoped to be in two years.

"I want to be working for *****, doing inpatient work, and for my personal life, engaged."

I asked Marie where she wanted to be in five years.

"Married and pregnant. Depends on whether or not I get burned out in this field. If I get burned out, I'll go to school. I won't be pregnant, but that can wait."

MIRA'S STORY

Knight Library, University of Oregon, Eugene, Oregon, Summer 2002

I became acquainted with Mira even before I started in the Program. We both attended a workshop on grief and dying just before the fall classes started. We talked many times before our first class and during lunch. Mira was fifty-five at the time of our interview. I started our interview with the question about her childhood.

"I was born in Eugene. My childhood was difficult. My dad was in the air force, and I went to different schools every two years. I flunked the third and fourth grades and hated school. I had really tough times. I think I have dyslexia, but I've never been formally diagnosed. I diagnosed myself. So that really hampered me and lowered my self-esteem.

"There were always changes that came on really fast. One Christmas my dad came home and said, 'We're moving, and the moving truck is right behind me.' We had a Christmas tree up, and we immediately took the decorations down and packed them. We gave the tree to a friend and neighbor. I remember being really, really upset that I wasn't able to tell my friends good-bye because we just up and left."

Mira then related some of the good times in her childhood.

"When I was about ten, we lived in Virginia, and my parents took us somewhere every weekend. We went to institutes and monuments all over Washington, D.C. and up and down into the Virginias. I was old enough to appreciate what I was seeing, and it really opened my world.

"My parents were so interested in our not being prejudiced. When I was little, I came in and asked my daddy what a 'nigger' was. He said, 'There are certain words we never use. That's one of them. Let's sit down and talk about some of the other ones.'

"In the military, you see and play with every color. So it was really nice that they wanted us to experience different cultures. It's helped me as an adult, but as a student in grade school and high school, I was very unhappy. I left school in the eleventh grade, did the *GED, and didn't come back until I was probably twenty-five."

Mira then talked about drugs and alcohol in her family and her relationships with her relatives.

"My grandparents on my father's side had problems. It skipped a generation. We'd see them every couple of years. They lived in Nebraska.

"Oregon was always our home residence, so we'd come and see relatives here. My family in Oregon is very small-minded and bigoted, and I have nothing in common with them at all. In fact, they've distanced themselves. Once my mother's little sister disowned us because we're not of her faith or her attitude. That's really sad, but bigotry is learned. My mother was able to leave and change.

"My mom is wonderful and very open-minded. In the military you'd meet so many people from different regions. She was always switching recipes and liked to go to different restaurants. We learned to go into nice restaurants and know different cultures."

We discussed Mira's own experiences with drugs and alcohol. She also talked about her 'different' life style.

"When I was a teenager, I'd binge drank a few times, mostly beer. Then I married an alcoholic. I wasn't even aware of these things at the time. During my pregnancy with my son, I didn't drink at all. Usually, I didn't drink unless the people around me drank.

"My husband was in Vietnam. When he came back, he was even more into alcohol. He got violent with me.

Within two years, I left and divorced him. I grew up while he was gone, but he regressed. I came back to Oregon and went to school for a couple of terms. I did go out and drink occasionally. I started to feel that *LCC and the college requirements were just too much.

"It was about 1971. There was a march against the war in Vietnam, so I got involved in the march. I'd been really interested in a sociology course that had talked about mob mentality. When I went into this march, I discovered mob mentality. I realized that had that mob run, I would have run with it. If they'd screamed, I'd have screamed. If somebody had thrown a rock, I would have too. I could see how easily a group of people could react, and it scared me to death.

"About that time, a friend turned me on to marijuana, hash, and then mescaline. I really enjoyed it. On my first date with my second husband, we did LSD together. He'd also gone through Vietnam. Soon we ran away together to the woods of Oregon and Washington. We camped out and picked apples. We enjoyed ourselves tremendously.

"My little boy was about four. I learned about bugs and polliwogs again, and we just had a great time. We filled our car and our little utility trailer with bedding and food and just took off. That whole summer, just getting in touch with nature and having fun with my son, was really a treat.

"We couldn't afford any drugs. I think maybe we took off with some, but they weren't a priority. We picked apples and that was it. This was the late sixties. Somewhere in there, we found the place to score, which was at an ice cream place in the outskirts of Yakima. We also bought a bag that was supposed to be marijuana, but it was an herb. You know, people get fooled and ripped off.

"We returned to Eugene, broke-up, and I went back to school. Still I was into alcohol and drugs, just enough to distract me. By spring, I was ready for change again. A man,

I'd spent the summer with, came back. So I cut loose and joined him. We stayed in California most of the summer and then came back to Oregon in the winter.

"I think that winter was a turning point in how I looked at drug use. The people who influenced me were not just, 'Let's party,' people. The party had ended. These people were what I would call early refugees from San Francisco and Los Angeles.

"A year or so later, I met other groups that came back from Chicago after the riot. People were moving to the West Coast to seek a calmer, gentler place to bring up their kids and to live. We were still under the threat of nuclear annihilation and the Vietnam war—all the scandal of the government and Nixon. It was an awful time.

"Those people who influenced me gave marijuana as a medicine. It was a communal thing. We would pass the peace pipe, so I learned to look at substances differently. I also learned a lot about natural food—all kinds of stuff that influence me to this day.

"And I got pregnant with my younger son and did a natural childbirth, which was wonderful. We really tried to pay attention and went into a more natural lifestyle. My partner was very supportive and was even ready to have the child at home, if necessary, because we lived way out of town. It was a pretty rough winter too.

"I wasn't into drugs in my pregnancy. I was being really good to myself. We moved into a school bus, which has a really neat story about where we lived and why we left. We got involved in living in the school bus and building a house truck.

"One time I got to sit and talk with one of the original people who created a house truck and is publishing a book about it. We talked about the times and how we wished we could do it all over again.

"It's wonderful to experience a lifestyle out of a desire to recycle. People threw away more things then. Some of the old trucks were really easy to fix. You just needed some basic wrenches and baling wire to fix a 1948 Dodge. Gas was twenty-five cents for a gallon, so we could live cheaply and comfortably.

"I was reminded of what a special time it was. Not much alcohol. Marijuana was a priority, but it wasn't a real priority. It was something nice to have, but it wasn't necessary. I had wine occasionally, and lots of folks would make their own. There were places we'd go where they grew marijuana. I think the alcohol and drugs did become compulsive for me.

"Probably around my thirties, I left the house truck, moved to Eugene, and lived there for thirteen years. During that time, I created and made beautiful clothes and did fairs, the Country Fair, and markets. I got off welfare, but learned how to keep track of things for low-income housing. You had to be accountable every month.

"In 1985, I married my best friend who is still my best friend. During our dating years, he introduced me to the Blues, to darts, and the bar scene, which I'd never been into before. Living out in the country, going to a bar was something new and exciting to me.

"So I started drinking more than ever. Then the recession hit tremendously hard for a lot of us, so that beer was the only thing we could afford. Marijuana was overpriced.

"My husband got a drunk-driving ticket and I'd added him to my car insurance. So I lost my insurance. We were just barely scraping by. He had to pay his fines and wouldn't admit that he'd done anything wrong. That infuriated me, so I basically kicked him out.

"I see him every year at the Country Fair and remind him that if I hadn't kicked him out, he never would have met his beautiful wife and had his three beautiful children. We laugh about it now. They're delightful people, and he's done really well for his family. I admire him.

"After our divorce, and my business started failing, it was basically one thing after another. My father was dying of cancer. I was very sick. I had another failed marriage. I was going downhill. I got involved with a man who was a drug dealer, a jerk, who hurt me a lot.

"I felt the world was so unjust to me. How can this man drive across town and make a hundred dollars, and I'm barely making money to pay utilities? He wouldn't contribute to helping me out. He just stayed with me. He couldn't see that he should contribute, so we came to an impasse. I kicked him out and just went into more alcohol.

"I know now that I had a major depression. I had no history of knowing what to do with depression. I was trying to medicate the pain of losses and changes. My son was graduating from high school. The new landlord wanted us to move, after thirteen years. Adding that to everything else, I was a basket case.

"Just about that time, I got a job, a really good job. Within a year I was able to apply for a recovery program that the insurance paid for. I kept the job, and they wanted me back after I did the program. My son had graduated and gone off to college. He was really worried about me. I never lost my home or my car. I still have my family. They have no idea!

"That was ten-and-a-half years ago. I look back and see that there are major turning points in people's lives: divorce, death in the family, all sorts of things. I had all of them, one after another, and they came at such a fast pace and just kept coming, I didn't know where to go for help, didn't have insurance, barely off welfare, just numb."

We talked about how she came into the Program and what her impressions were.

"My good job lasted about five-and-a-half years. Then I had tendonitis really bad and had to resign. I met another 'crafts' person, moved out into the country, worked on crafts for a few years, and really enjoyed it. Again, I was back in my comfort zone of wearing long skirts and eating lots of vegetables.

"A number of times I had been asked by several people about recovery. They asked me such questions as 'What do you do?' and 'How did you help yourself?' Several people talked about how they were not going to make it unless their partner changed.

"I kept getting all these inquiries, and I'd heard that LCC had this Program. It just kept coming up. I'd think about it when I got up in the morning. I'd think about it when I was driving. Finally, I got the paperwork and looked into it. I applied to the Program at LCC and was accepted. I feel as if I have a calling for the work.

"So within a year I was surprised that I was getting good grades, keeping up with the material, and loving the Program, the people, and the teachers.

"My internship was a disaster. I have a different work ethic. I'd rather be a bag lady than let a company buy me. And there was a lot of 'Let's go in and play the game of trying to look busy.'

"I couldn't do that. I'd had my own business for a long time in my home. It was nothing for me to work twelve hours, fourteen hours to get ready for a show or to finish a wedding dress. So, to go in for eight hours a day and for five of them look busy. I can't do that. My experience with ***** was quite interesting.

"It was one thing after another. And I thought, 'If they treat their clients the way they're treating me, it's a wonder that they still have open doors.'

"It's a control thing. They can control you and are able to play you for several months because you think you might get a job there.

"It's a power thing. My best buddy, *****, told me horror stories of how the people at her internship facility were treated.

"I went in as an intern and wanted to look around. What I found, when I looked around, was appalling. The way they were treating their counselors and their attitudes towards their clients were not good at all. It was like an assembly line.

"***** is hiring a woman who has a degree in English. She's never read a book or paper that talked about drug use or the paperwork. I know paperwork is the biggest thing. It's almost as if she were being set up for failure.

"A lot of the clients there were mandated. They were losing their kids. They were going to go to jail. I felt that the administration was more interested in getting the money than in treating people. So I learned a lot and decided to go on to school.

"I started looking at alternatives. I really like school. I got accepted at family and human services here at the University of Oregon, but I'm not sure that's what I'm going to do. I think again, about the requirements for continuing volunteer work with fancy names like *Practicum, but it means working for free for another two years.

"I can understand the reason for that. Seventy-five percent of the students accepted in this program are under twenty-five. I can understand that having them learn as volunteer workers is important, but I've done it forever."

Mira spoke about an alternate internship that attracted her.

"One administrator has been involved in the 'Culture Jam' at the Oregon Country Fair. It's for kids, fourteen to eighteen, a week-long camp-out at that beautiful property. They're going to have musicians, artists, activists, and teachers. A wonderful time! Vegetarian food! A lot of their parents grew up at the Country Fair. So I'm going to help with that one.

"I told the administrator that I'd rather give my time to the Country Fair, which is a nonprofit organization than to go into an organization where administrators are paid big, huge bucks, but they depend on free labor.

"So I'd rather do that and be a part of the culture, the art culture. It was a place where I learned about drugs and did too many, and then left drugs. Four years ago, they made the Country Fair an alcohol- and drug-free event. It's wonderful—everybody, the environment, the focus of the fair. They also give a lot of money to the schools. That's where I want to go. That's where I'll work for nothing."

I asked Mira for her thoughts on the Chemical Dependency Program at Lane.

"I was told at the very beginning what I was going to do. I learned everything I needed to learn to take the test, the state certification test. Ruth was always right up front, 'You can do this, you can do that.' The teachers are, for the most part, exceptional human beings.

"What I learned goes along with what I learned as an intern. This field is not ready for exceptional people like me. What I learned here was an extraordinary experience. I think I'll carry this, the camaraderie and the courage that I gained, courage that I never dreamed of. I'm not sure how that came about. I felt that no matter where I turned at Lane, if I asked for help, I would receive it.

"It was so smooth and wonderful. I wish there was more communication between the programs in the community and our Program because they've missed out on some really great people who went though this Program."

We then talked about some of the things Mira wants to do and where she'd like to be ten years from now.

"I'd like to get involved in putting together a how-to book about the way I've learned to live. And how more and more people are forced to live a simpler, lifestyle. Enthusiasm and silly enthusiasm can make somebody's day. The Country Fair means so much to me. I can just see the ten years whizzing by.

"I'm going on for the Bachelor's Degree, and I might go into computer science—maybe a Master's. I don't know, but I love school. To work part-time with a nonprofit organization sounds good. And maybe teaching, doing workshops. I want to keep my integrity and not buy into the system for money or do anything that's against my integrity.

"I have hope for the future and the Program. I think people like you and I realize that the administration and the money are getting in the way of helping people. We want this to work and see that the need is so great. I think there's enough caring people, who are ready to be educated, so I hold out hope for the future."

PATRICIA'S STORY

Cafeteria, Lane Community College, Eugene, Oregon. Summer 2002

Patricia and I have been friends for about fifteen years. We both taught adult education classes for Lane Community College in Florence, Oregon. We worked together on some community projects, and we always had fun together. I thought I knew everything about her, but discovered much more in this interview.

"I thought I wanted to be a nun and take care of old people and orphans. I was thinking very seriously about it, but the Little Sisters Of the Poor rejected me. I think they thought I was too young, and I think my mother might have had something to do with it. After that I was walking to school one day with my books, and *****from up the street offered to carry my books and started following me around. My mother said I've been boy crazy ever since.

"I got to stay with my grandmother, so I could finish high school. It was a most lenient situation. She was an unconditional-love grandma, and she'd always say, 'Patricia, let's put on the tea.' She'd shuffle down the long hallway to put on the tea, and there was a pathway in the linoleum from my grandmother's shuffling. I remember that my grandmother was always old, with a bun, a black dress, and those big heels like the nuns.

"But I noticed boys and got to hang out with my friends. I was drinking, not a lot. I always felt as a child that because I saw my father drink that I would never grow up and be like that. I would be different.

"I remember tasting liquor at Irish christenings and holidays, and I remember liking to play when my father would take us up and down Amsterdam Avenue to the Irish bars. My father would say, 'Don't tell your mother because

I'm supposed to be taking you to Central Park.' Since I was the oldest, I took care of the younger ones.

"We were burnt out of our house twice, and the ceiling fell in. I remember my grandfather, who had a special pass because he'd been a bus conductor, would come on Sundays afternoons and take me to the main bus station, He'd, say, 'Which bus do you want to take?' I could pick a bus and we could go anywhere. It was a real treat, and he was a special part of my life."

We paused for a moment. Then Patricia told me about some of her early 'adventures' in the world of alcohol and drugs.

"I guess I started drinking after graduation from eighth grade. In high school, it was on the sneak, and my friends and I would hang out. It was the secret world that my family and the nuns didn't know about. My friends and I would have drinks, and I'd get in trouble for staying out too late.

"My parents never discussed it except for the high school prom. I drank quite a bit. The next morning my mother said, 'Well, that was different because it was graduation.' I thought it was unnatural because she was so strict. It was really strange. She gave me tomato juice and laughed about it, as if it were an expected right of passage.

"She didn't know that my boyfriend in the air force couldn't get leave to take me to the prom. A friend at the all-girls academy was from an Italian family, and I used to go visit them. It seems my friend's family was somehow involved with the 'mob' even though they don't call it that anymore. So she had this young uncle who volunteered to take me.

"I had this really fancy dress that looked like Cinderella with lace and pink rosettes, and I wore a rhinestone crown. We went to the prom, and afterwards he took me to his friend's house. She turned out to be a jazz singer who hung out with the 'mob.' She looked me over and said that they couldn't take me to places in my prom dress.

"She loaned me one of her outfits—a black jersey sheath with long sleeves and a plunging neckline. At the hemline was a three-inch fox fur that wrapped around to a point over the knee, and with that came a big black stole. Of course, I put the hair up and took off the crown. There I was, barely seventeen, in this outfit, drinking in nightclubs and after-hours places.

"At one place, Jerry Vale was singing, and my friend introduced me to a lot of 'family.' The really funny part was that right after we left, there was a big shooting where they sprayed and shot a few of the mob bosses. So at seventeen and with a few drinks, I was already off to a roaring start. So that was the beginning of mob connections as a young woman and drinking."

We paused and Patricia started laughing before she continued.

"I also had a run-in with the law. For some reason, and I'm still amazed, my parents got me a Buick convertible. I was driving down a main street in New Jersey, and a police car made a U-turn and hit me broadside. Why they didn't have their lights on, I don't know. Anyway I ended up in the hospital with a concussion and a broken nose. But the police didn't take me to the hospital first. They took me to the jail. This was New Jersey in the fifties.

"An old couple showed up and said they'd been on the avenue and saw the police car hit me. Then the police took me to the hospital. But later they arrested me about some traffic tickets that they said I hadn't paid and put me in jail.

"There I was in jail. I called the 'uncle' who had taken me to the prom, my boyfriend, who was in trouble for drugs in that town, and a big 'Labor Boss,' whom I was dating. All three called the jail and wanted to post the bail.

"The police said, 'Oh my God, what have we here? She knows a mob boss and a labor boss!' The mob boss came down with the cash and the police said, 'We can't do it because the chief's not here to sign off for it.' So they kept me over the weekend. It was miserable there.

"The cops would come to the outer door of my cell and harass me. They gave me one bologna sandwich, and the blankets were scratchy. Anyway, the mob boss came with the cash when the weekend was over. I think there was some calls from some higher-ups because later I got a personal phone call and an apology from the mayor of that town. So that was my run-in with the law at eighteen."

We then discussed Patricia's modeling and acting career.

"I modeled as a young child. Then I did modeling in New York and started making money. I'd do the boat shows at Madison Square Garden as a model/rep person. I met many famous people, and there were men around 'modeling' who had lots and lots of money.

"I was introduced to marijuana at a friend's house in the late fifties or early sixties. I remember people were starting to say, 'Well, we aren't juicers.' One horrible night we went to an apartment to get a little grass. There were some side rooms and dark lighting, and some people were starting to use needles and shooting up.

"Another couple came home with us. The two guys went into the bathroom, and I wondered why they were in there so long. I got very concerned and checked. They had both overdosed. My girlfriend and I spent the night pouring water over their faces to revive them. It was quite a night. I kept waiting for the defining moment of when to call a doctor friend.

"I think that's when I knew for the first time that I was in trouble. I was probably twenty because I used to have to put things in my boyfriend's name because I wasn't twenty-one, even though I was making good money as a model.

"We broke-up and made-up several times. Then he said, 'Well, the thing for us is to get married and move to California.' That settled me down for a while, being married and working at the movie studios. We monitored our drinking and grass smoking, but that marriage broke-up. I'm sure alcohol and drugs had something to do with it. But it was mainly that he took me for granted, and I caught him cheating."

Patricia went on to talk about her life as a single person in California.

"I went back full time to acting and studying acting. Sometimes I would model. I did modeling for some of the department stores. I'm not tall like the fashion models, but I've always done sportswear for the catalogs.

"I was dating musicians and actors. There was a long period in the sixties when I was living with a rock musician. That time was the experimental hippie era, so there was a period of psychedelics, LSD, peyote, and all those things. I did all of them! I never missed any of them!

"After that was another whole story. There was an Oscar-winning screenplay writer who had a yacht and a Ferrari. There were expensive wines and brandies, and we did grass and cocaine. I would arrange parties on the boat with famous producers, directors, models, female agents, and actresses and jet off to locations with movie stars."

I asked Patricia if she'd been happy during that time.

"No, I was acting a role. I was acting out. I thought it was fun and transitory, but I thought that that was what I was supposed to do to be happy.

"I decided I wanted to settle down a bit. I was dating a doctor and was really fond of his children. He had a horse ranch, rode on an English hunt, and lived out of town. I thought it would be a good thing for me. It turned out to be the worst of the worst. He drank heavier than anyone I'd ever been involved with before.

"We drank, we smoked pot, and he'd also been into the psychedelics. On top of that, he introduced me to the wonderful world of prescription drugs. That was his answer to everything—take a pill."

We talked about how Patricia got turned around.

"My husband wasn't coming home. A friend of mine—a jazz singer, who'd been married to a famous bandleader, had been over to my house. She'd seen how my husband's behavior deteriorated as he drank, became rude, and embarrassed me.

"Anyway she knew my husband wasn't coming home because he was out partying. Here I was at home, playing 'Mrs. Doctor' and raising his children. She said she was going to this meeting and wanted me to go too. In my mind, I really thought I was being supportive of her. I felt 'the poor thing.' I liked her so much, and she was having all these problems with alcoholism in her family. I could relate to that. My father was an alcoholic.

"So I went to an Al-Anon meeting that night, and there was a young doctor who talked about being the oldest child in an alcoholic family. He was telling my story—a male version of my story."

We talked more about how Patricia got turned around.

"So from that day in 1977 to this, even before I got sober in 1982, I've been involved in twelve-step programs. I had nothing better to do. I had all the money and time in the world. I'd get all dressed up in my designer clothes, show up at an Al-Anon meeting, and cry my eyes out. I'd leave, change my clothes, and go to another meeting. I'd go to several meetings a day. I did that for years and became very active in Al-anon.

"In Al-Anon, some of the ladies said they'd love me until I could learn to love myself. They also said it would be a good thing to learn more about my husband by going to an A.A. meeting. I figured that if these women could get their men to stop drinking, I could get my husband to mind me.

"I didn't care if he drank a little at home if I could get him to mind. I even sought out a sponsor in Al-Anon. The sponsor was also married to a doctor, whom she got sober. I figured that she could teach me how to do this right, but that didn't work out."

Patricia paused and asked, "Do you want to hear the story about trying to run over my husband with a car. Of course, I said yes.

"I was in alone at night. We had a legal separation. The judge put him in the guesthouse. In those days, in Southern California, the separated couples lived in different parts of the house because they couldn't divide the property. He was living in the guesthouse, and I was in the front house. I was living with drawn drapes—crazed and obsessed.

"I was preparing to go to my Al-Anon meeting that I was leading. I was in my car. My husband came around in the circular driveway of our house on Sunset Boulevard. He locked the fences and wanted to talk to me.

"I had a gun under the seat, but I didn't even think about it at the time. He tried to open the door and drag me out of the car. I got the car door closed, but he wouldn't open the gate. So I backed the car, put it in drive, and aimed at him. He ran across the lawn.

"I felt like I was in a James Bond movie. I was the good guy, and he was the bad guy. It was self-defense. I was aiming the car at him, and, all of a sudden, it occurred to me in a brilliant stroke of genius and enlightenment—that when the police came, they'd see the tire imprints from my 'beamer,' and they'd know it was me.

"So I backed up, and he opened the gate. I drove to the police station and wrote out a report. Then I went to Al-anon, led the meeting, and shared. I told them just what happened. I thought they'd be shocked and horrified. I was being honest, as they had encouraged me. They said that this was 'progress not perfection,' and that I was progressing. I'd showed up in Al-Anon originally suicidal. Now I'd become homicidal and that was progress."

I asked Patricia if she'd followed the advice of her Al-Anon friends.

"I started going to A.A. to learn about the alcoholic. One day I was having a particularly bad day at the house in Brentwood on Sunset Boulevard and called the A.A. office. I told the person that answered that I didn't understand my life.

"I'm married to this doctor who's handsome and talented. I have this big house, a Mercedes, and all the others in the garage, but two of them are in the shop. I have plumbers digging up the front lawn, and the washing machine is broken. I just don't understand what is wrong or why my life isn't working.

"So she said to me. 'Get right over here. I understand how you feel.' So I immediately asked her to be my sponsor. She sounded to me as if she had red hair and was hot stuff. She turned out to be a blond who spent most of her life at Gucci's on Rodeo Dive and drove a Mercedes. She was a piece of work, a real character, and a good friend.

"I started going to A.A. meetings with her, especially the women's A.A. meeting. I found such great strength with the wonderful women there. But I couldn't identify myself as an alcoholic. I was still in Al-Anon, and this friend helped me a great deal.

"After I got divorced, I moved to Malibu and started writing stuff for documentary filmmaking. I was back to work, doing some acting and some modeling. I started writing for local cable TV women's shows. I was the hostess of the show, wrote, and indirectly produced it, so that was fun. When I got my divorce settlement, I traveled all over the world.

"Then I was back living in Malibu and wondering about my friend, *****. We'd been at the Actor's Studio together and studied with Lee Strasberg. We'd played brother and sister together on the stage, in film, and on television. He was a director, actor, and a famous choreographer. He was working in New York.

"So I tracked him down, found his number, and called him backstage just before he was about to go on. He said, 'Leave it to you. I want to talk to you about something.' And he said, 'You've been going to all these meetings and seem to be so much better since your divorce. I wonder if you'd take me to some of those meetings.'

"I invited him to come and stay with me. He came and said he was getting off cocaine and went with me to some Al-Anon meetings. I thought if I could get him to A.A., I could help him.

"I contacted *****, a retired schoolteacher, who calls himself a nature cat. We used to go on hikes together. People thought that he was left over from the hippie era, but he was long before the hippies. He was a beat from the beat generation.

"I knew he went to Al-Anon and also to A.A. A person who did both was called a double winner and illustrated the A.A. saying that people came in the back door through Al-Anon. I introduced him to my actor friend. My actor friend started attending A.A. meetings too.

"My beat friend and I went on a hike on July 4, 1982, and we talked about our actor friend. And my beat friend said, 'Well, our friend's already going to A.A. meetings, but what about you?' I asked him what he meant.

"We started talking and relating stories about our hippie days and how we drank and used. We were way up on a cliff overlooking the ocean, watching fireworks. I know I sounded just like someone in A.A. telling her story. I had always used all these excuses: 'It was my dad. It was my boyfriend. It was my husband, and we had to entertain and have the best wines.'

"I gave all these reasons, and ***** said the following words to me, which sound so trite, but they hit me right behind the eyes, 'You know, eagles fly with eagles.' So I asked him how I would know if I were an alcoholic.

"He informed me that there was a test. I replied, 'You mean, I've been in Al-Anon all these years, and there's a test. No one ever told me.'

"The test was for thirty days. You had to have the same drink at the same time every day for thirty days, 'No problem,' I said, and we went back to the house and set up the test. I couldn't do it and said, 'Okay, forget it. I'll just go to A.A. for thirty days.'

"So I was going to A.A. saying, 'I'm an alcoholic,' but feeling that I was a spy at A.A. meetings. I went to one meeting, and a woman said to me, 'You're new, aren't you?' She asked me a very impertinent question, 'Are you an alcoholic?' I fumbled and muttered, 'I don't know.' She said, 'Oh come on and be one. It's a lot of fun.' So from that day, July 4, 1982, I haven't had a drink or drug."

We then discussed the deaths of Patricia's mom and many of her friends. She took care of ***** before his death from AIDS. And she had a glamorous job working for a studio.

"I had many friends, a number of close friends who died from AIDS—so much death, dying, and going to funerals. I was working my way up as an up-and-coming female studio executive, but I was working long hours. I was still going to meetings and had friends, but I didn't have much free time. I felt no pleasure in my life.

"A friend had moved to Oregon, and he invited me to his wedding. I helped with the wedding, did the flowers, some cooking, and baking. I made all the floral arrangements and bouquets for twelve bridesmaids. They invited me for Thanksgiving. I was thinking about a bed-and–breakfast on the Oregon Coast. I figured that a change in careers and in my life would be good at this time.

"So I came up here, and naturally being a member of A.A., I wanted to go to a meeting. I dragged my friend all over Florence in the rain, trying to find a meeting. We finally found it with old guys smoking. They all looked to me as if they had raincoats on. The coffee pot was gurgling.

"I was the only woman at the meeting that night. I walked in with a cape and boots from Italy and wearing a hat. I sat down and bumped into the person next to me, and he apologized for it, even though I was the one who did the bumping. He was tall and handsome.

"It was a study meeting. He passed me the A.A. book, and I'm checking him out. He had on a flannel shirt and jeans. I thought, 'Oh my, God, a logger. How much would I have in common with him?'

"He didn't have a wedding band, and I looked down and saw he had designer sneakers on. I thought that looked like Southern California.

"We went for coffee and found out that we were the same age, born and raised within a few blocks of each other in New York City. The rest is history! We just celebrated twelve years of a happy marriage!

"We decided from the first that we both had our own programs, but that we'd be loving and supporting of each other. We've been committed that way. He respects and appreciates my working with others. He encourages it and is very supportive about me going back to school and my new career."

Patricia and I talked about the Chemical Dependency Program and how she became involved in it.

"This friend of mine, Jan, always said it was something I might do. I had another friend, who was eighty years old with twenty-seven years of sobriety. She said that she was too old to do it, but I was the one who could.

"When I showed up for the first class, I felt that I was home and that I'd arrived, the same way I've felt about twelve-step programs. It was perfect and natural. I wanted to know more about alcohol and addiction. I wanted to be smarter, more intelligent, and professional.

"I felt I had so much to contribute, and it was the same as in my theater days. I was always ready to jump in, participate, and play my part. I felt that I had a lot to offer and a lot to learn. It's been stimulating and natural. I've always felt I was in the right place."

We then discussed the hardest things for her in the Program.

"The first thing was living up to my own standards and maintaining my 'A's.' I've had a four-point since I got here. The other thing was worrying about the finances. My husband got kidney cancer just before I went to school. Going to school was another thing that I felt that I really had to do because if he had a recurrence, or if he didn't get better, I might need to take care of him. I needed to work and have a profession that would pay well and have hospitalization and other benefits."

For my final question, I asked Patricia where she hoped to be in the future, two or five years from now.

"I don't know—wherever my path takes me. I would like to continue my schooling. I'd like to be working professionally, but I'm sure I'll learn more in my new program at the University of Oregon.

"I have ideas about designing prevention programs. I still like working with adults who are in treatment. I have a number of ideas that I've discussed with the psychologist, who worked at the facility where I interned and later worked. I've ideas that would incorporate programs that I've designed for children using my theater arts background."

LOUANNE'S STORY

Patio, Knight Library, University of Oregon, Eugene, Oregon, Spring 2002

When we all gathered for breakfast before our first classes, LouAnne always had her biking gear with her. She and Mike both rode up the Thirtieth Street hill on their bicycles. Most of us had "junk" food for breakfast, but LouAnne always had healthy snacks that she brought from home. She never talked a lot about herself, but was always ready to listen to others. After this interview I felt that I knew a great deal more about her.

My first question was about her childhood.

"My parents joined a nonprofit when I was a year old. It was called the Institute of Cultural Affairs, and it meant that we moved to the ghetto. My dad was a Presbyterian minister in a little church, and my parents decided that they needed to save the world. That was the beginning of not having much contact with them and being cared for by a rotation of people who were a part of the organization.

"Now both my older sister and I are benefiting at this point in our lives because my parents edit my papers at the drop of a hat or help me to write a proposal for a scholarship. They also take care of my sister's two-year-old son. Whereas, when we were kids, they were on call twenty-four hours a day for the organization for different reasons. We basically had one day and one evening with our parents. So it was an interesting childhood, for sure.

"It was inner-city Chicago, and it was pretty grim. I remember we'd all walk in a group to school when I was in first grade—all those little, tiny first-graders—and there'd be drunks on the pavement. Parental protection would have been nice. We didn't have it, but we did have other people. It was a big organization. Many were good people, and some weren't good people. You're going to have both. To be fair, I'd have to say that the good people had bad aspects too.

"Umm. Did I like school? Well, you see, I didn't have a home to go back to, so yeah, I liked school. If I'd had a home, that I wanted to stay at rather than going to school, I might not have liked school so much. I did well and was liked by my teachers. That made life easier."

We talked about the degree alcoholism played in her childhood and about all the places she lived as a child.

"My parents weren't alcoholics or addicts, but there were people in the organization who were. It didn't necessarily affect me directly. I had several good friends who had an alcoholic for a parent rather than having one myself. We were in Stockton, California, Talent, Georgia, and New York. Then we were on the west side of Chicago when I was five, and the north side of Chicago when I was six. From eight to ten, I was in San Antonio. When I was eleven, I was in Africa for a year with my parents.

"I was with them more often in Africa, but they were still really, really busy, and I was focused on school. I don't remember doing a lot of things with my parents, but I do remember having a holiday when we went to Tanzania and Botswana on the train.

"I like my parents. They're good people, but I would never have raised my children like that. And I didn't raise my children in that way. I can see that I wouldn't be who I am today, had my childhood not happened that way, so I'm glad it happened. I don't feel damaged anymore from that. I'm very emotional. It took a lot of recovering from that neglect, or whatever you want to call it, and the other stuff that went down in the organization too."

I asked Lou about her high school experiences.

"I never was a 'crowd' kind of person. My first stint at high school was in Memphis, Tennessee. I had one friend in the whole school. He was a black guy, and he didn't fit in either because he wasn't in one of the social classes. He wasn't poor black or rich black, and he wasn't poor white or rich white. I didn't fit into them either and I refused to. I wouldn't wear certain clothing or allow myself to merge into just one crowd.

"I used to party on the weekends even though I was a devoted student. When I was in Memphis, I had a boyfriend, four years older than me. We did a lot of partying on the weekends. My friend, Randy, was very into drugs and alcohol. Through him, I met his friend, John, and we were tight. I remember taking speed on Monday mornings in order to do the day. I remember gym class as being really fun.

"Then I moved to Houston and didn't party as much because my boyfriend wasn't there. We got to be friends with a teacher that we used to go to bars with. Yeah, she was great, 'perfect' for us. My tendency was always to use as much as I could and get really blitzed. I never drank or used with the intention of getting just a 'little' buzz."

Lou and I discussed her marriage and her children who are in Ireland with their father.

"My marriage broke up in Ireland. I did professional psychotherapy training for about three-and-a-half years. I moved to England with my daughter and practiced there. Then I worked as a contractor with my partner here for about four years."

Lou spoke about how she became clean and sober.

"I was in London. I probably smoked pot a couple of times there, didn't drink a lot, but I started smoking cigarettes again. I remember drinking a four-pack, the tall ones, and my partner really didn't like me drinking. I didn't do it very often. It was, 'I just need to check out for a little bit.' I think it got worse about the time when I was going to leave England and come back to the U.S.

"That was really scary for me to leave there and come back here. When I came back, I pretty much quit everything. I stopped smoking. My family never drank the way I did. They would have a beer, but I didn't want just one beer. I always wanted more. I decided it was just better to have something else.

"My partner was already in A.A. He's not actually an alcoholic, but a marijuana addict. His sponsor happened to be in A.A., and that worked for him. I actually attended meetings for four years.

"There seemed to be a spiritual center, which helped because my son was living in Ireland. That was really hard for me. It was hard for me to trust that there was a spiritual path for me. It always comes back to that. My journey has always been a spiritual one. When my son stayed in Ireland, I was pretty much on the floor. It's like I was a puddle on the floor. I had to pull myself up to be a mom for my daughter."

We discussed how Lou got into the Counselor Training Program.

"I'd done the psychotherapy training in England. A friend of mine was doing the Chemical Dependency Counselor Training. The year before, I did a guided self-healing with my mom. I'd been working, doing contracting with my partner, but therapy has always been my true love.

"I love the work and the Program offered an opportunity to get back in and do it, get into the work as I saw it. Also, because of my childhood, drug addiction and incarceration have always bothered me. Living in a nonprofit in the ghetto, I just wanted there to be justice. I wanted there to be something humane, and I think this Program was a bridge to answer all those things."

I asked LouAnne to talk about the hardest thing for her in the Program.

"I don't think there was anything really hard about it. If there was a difficulty, it was that it wasn't challenging enough. And yet I think that's what I needed. I think it was a bridge for me to get into school and to get where I am now.

It helped people. Ruth is really good at holding people. I think she held all the people in the Program and is the reason that people didn't drop out.

"I think I needed that. I think I benefited from what she provided in holding that space and from her inspiration too. And I think that I benefited from her attitude about the poor. It fit right into my belief system, and it was affirming for me to have a professor saying all those things that I felt were true."

We talked about LouAnne's interning experiences.

"I interned at the jail, and that was perfect. The reason it was perfect was because the supervisor let me have complete reign. She could see that I knew what I was doing. She was overwhelmed with her own stuff. She trusted my ethics, so she just got out of the way and let me go for it, which isn't surprising in the chemical dependency field. It wouldn't have worked if she had tried to supervise me more stringently. It would have been much more difficult for both her and me.

"At my other internship, I didn't learn shit. All I learned about was paperwork. Because of my background of growing up in a nonprofit, I'd facilitated groups as a kid. It wasn't difficult for me. When I was working at that other internship, I can't tell you how bored I was. It's just completely boring for me to teach information. That's not my thing.

"So I was working at level two with a criminal group. It was grim. The counselor before me was a power and control freak, and those guys were just ready to sink their teeth into whomever came into the door. I remember the first group that I led, and what I did for a check-in. I had them choose an animal and a color that they identified with. It was cool. I wasn't going to come in there pretending to be a regular ***** counselor. I was going to come there in full color regalia.

"It did deteriorate over time because I'm a soft touch. That's how I raise my children. That's how I lead my life and communicate with people. I'm very emotional, and I see where others are.

"I think that boundaries are really important, don't get me wrong. I keep good boundaries with my children and with my groups too. This was my first group, and they had me for lunch. The talk about women got worse over time, and finally I had to ask someone to leave. I felt really beat-up by —whatever—just their attitude toward women. I had a lot on at school and was working too much.

"I had to ask someone to leave. He got angry at a comment that another man had made and said, 'Why don't you——my——?' I just said, 'You need to go.' So he left and everything quieted down after that.

"Then I did the *****, and a job came up at *****. I didn't have time to take it. And once I started at the University of Oregon, I couldn't do everything I wanted to.

"I do have an energy psych group for women who are a support group for each other. I'm training them to run their own group. It's just in town with women I've been working with for years through the jail. There are some new people coming, but mostly people I've worked with in the past."

I asked Lou to explain more about energy psychology.

"Energy psychology is using the meridians of the body to address what's going on when you have a thought, say about a traumatic memory, you can feel it in your body. It's also sitting here right in your field, in your energetic field.

"So if you address your meridian system, electrical system, and electro-shock therapy, you're relaxing that system. You open up channels. You're relaxing that system. That relaxes your body and addresses you physically, mentally, and emotionally. The precursor for energy psych is *rapid eye. They've done the research necessary for proof. Energy psych hasn't done that yet."

I asked LouAnne where she hoped to be in five years.

"Five years? That's a good question. I want to be teaching at a university level. I'm not completely sure about that. I think I have to go through a Master's Degree program to know whether I'm willing to do a Ph.D. and whether I have the funding for it. I think I've been resisting the temptation to go to school my whole life. I don't want to go through that much school, or pay that much money in order to do what I already know how to do. There's nothing wrong with more education. I always learn more. I always get more tools.

"But I've been resisting a long time, and part of the reason is that I want to go all the way, as far as I can go, and I don't know whether I can get there or not. I also think that meridian or energy psychology therapy addresses issues so well and is so effective. It's a combination of things. If I don't bring it into the prisons, if I don't teach it, who's going to? Because energy psych is on the fringe. It's not central at all.

"Where do I want to be in my personal life? I don't know. I want to be closer to my kids. They're on the other side of the ocean, and I usually only see them once a year for a couple of months. We're very tight, and I talk to them all the time.

"It was lot harder, but it's gotten easier. It's interesting. Things happen, and life changes. I don't think I really thought about going back to England until this scholarship came across and then I think, 'Well, even without a scholarship, maybe I should go, just go, so I can be with my kids.'

"I'd leave my partner here. He and I both have debts. He has more debts than I do, but we've got debts together too. He's got something going now where he might be able to pay it off. Our relationship's not the same as most people's. I don't know that we can survive being away for years with me living in England.

"My life isn't about my relationship. My life is about my kids and my work. He's a great guy. It's not that I want to leave him. It's just that I want to do other things. It would be harder if he were a different person, but he's just empowered me. He said, 'What scares me about you going over there is that you might want to live there.'

"I thought about that all day. When I came home in the evening, I asked him if he wanted to go to England with me. He said, 'I'm going to be a grandpa in Portland. No, I'm not coming.' That's the reality. We met each other after we both already had children. We're really good for each other. I'll miss him. He's the person I think I needed, and the relationship just strengthens me to this day."

My final question to Lou was, "Do you have anything to add before I turn off the recorder?

"Hmm. Have I anything I want to add? Well! I think about the ghetto, and I think about this society and how hypocritical it is. There's such a cultural milieu and a belief system that you can do whatever you want in America, you just have to work hard enough. I think that's the biggest crock of bullshit I've ever heard.

"I've lived in England, and they take care of their people a lot better than they do here. I know it's gotten worse since the Thatcher regime. But they still take care of their people a lot better than we do here. Here it's scary for everybody. It's not just terrifying for the homeless person. It's chilling for every part of society because there's nothing to catch you if you fall.

"It might not be that frightening for the middle-and-upper class, but everyone else is living hand-to-mouth and there is nothing. You lose your job, and you don't have enough money for food for the kids. People say that you can get free food in Lane County, there's plenty of food. It's like 'bull shit.' There's never enough. So I guess that's what I would say.

"If in ten years time, I'm back here, that's what I'm hoping. That my experience over there might give a sense of how this could change because this is my country. I don't want to leave it and say it's obviously because it's too tough back here. It's not my way to say 'I don't want to be where it's tough because I can't take it.' That's really not what I want to do. That's not how I want to lead my life.

"I can't tell you how much better I feel doing human services in any form in England compared to here. At least, the people there have something to fall on. At least, the people have housing, food, and options. They're a respectable part of society even though they don't have employment. That's big! So that would be my last comment."

PAUL'S STORY

Continental Deli, Eugene, Oregon, Winter 2003

Paul and I met at the Deli early in the morning because it was close to his internship, and he was scheduled for a training program right after we finished the interview. It was much quieter than the LCC cafeteria and is one of my favorite breakfast places.

Paul could have been a model for men's clothes. He always dressed well, and, of course, we all gave him a hard time about it. Paul liked to joke. Since he usually sat behind me, he'd crack me up as much as Marty did, and again the instructor always looked at me. We always had fun.

Paul discussed his childhood and his family.

"I grew up in San Francisco. I was born in '62. My mother and I lived in the projects because my mother and father got divorced. Then my stepfather came, and we moved into a regular house. He was a mailman. Around 1970, we moved into our first house. It was up on this big hill in San Francisco.

"From the balcony, I could see Candlestick Park. I could look across the Bay and see the Oakland Coliseum. I could look a little to my left and see the Bay Bridge. A little to the left of that, I could see the Transamerica Building. You've seen pictures of that pyramid building. I could see that from my balcony."

I asked him how alcohol played a part in his life.

"My stepfather was an alcoholic. I think just about every day he and a few of his buddies would get off work, come over, drink beer, and play dominoes. My mom never drank or smoked."

I asked Paul what he remembered about his early school years.

"I remember kindergarten. Five of us lived on the same block, and we'd walk to the top of the block. When I first started going to school, the Zodiac killer was out in San Francisco. Remember him? We were scared because we walked up the street to the street at the top, and went down another street. It was foggy the first thing in the morning. We walked hand in hand, scared to death.

"When I was six, my mother didn't want me to go to that school anymore. She wanted me to go to another school. So she taught me how to walk to a bus stop. That was before child molesters were snatching kids and all that kind of stuff. I'd catch a city bus for about ten blocks. Then I'd catch another for about ten blocks, and then, I'd get on the school bus and ride to school. I was six!"

Paul talked about his mother's conversion to the Jehovah Witness religion.

"That changed the whole dynamic for the family. When I was eight, she said, 'This is your last Christmas.' My stepfather tried it too, but he didn't like it. That was when the family went separate ways. But I liked school. I was just mad and always in trouble.

"At about eight years old, I found out that my father wasn't my real father. He was my stepfather. My father came to town from Chicago, and we met over at my aunt's house. The next time that I saw my dad, I was twelve. He came to my school. He wore this business suit, and they pulled me from class. I guess my mother must have set it up because my stepfather didn't want him to come to our house.

"When he came in and I saw him, I was like, 'Don't take me, mister! I didn't do anything! I didn't do anything.' Then he told me who he was. I don't know who I thought he was. I was only twelve."

Then Paul talked about his high school years.

"In the ninth grade, I was bad. I was what you would call incorrigible. I woke up one Saturday morning and it's the police. My mother and stepfather had called the police on me. So I got put in a boy's school. I did my whole ninth grade in Palm Springs at *****, in the middle of the desert.

"They had it divided up into age groups with six clubs or sections. It was like this big old hotel. It was okay. Then I got back into public school. I scored really high in the ninth grade on tests and placement tests.

"I went to this high school on the other side of town. My mother didn't want me going to the school just two blocks away. She said, 'You know all these kids. You grew up with them. I don't care where you go, but you are not going to that school.'

"So I chose a school on the other side of town called Abraham Lincoln School. I got off to a bad start. High school was fun for me. I used to cut and stuff. I didn't realize until the first day of twelfth grade that I needed every single credit to graduate with the twelfth grade. I really worked because I wanted to graduate with my class, and I did.

"I think I had my first drink at about twelve. Eleventh grade is when I started drinking. I went to live with my cousins, and they lived in a different part of town. They were a little rich. It was a four-story house, and we lived in an apartment in the basement. The three of us shared an apartment. We went to school, sang in the choir, and played sports.

"Then I went to City College and then to San Francisco State. A friend of mine wrote, 'Paul, you need to come up to Oregon because it's different here. Nobody's getting killed up here, no crime, and no burglary.'

"So I came up. I was supposed to be here at eight o'clock in the morning, but I showed at three o'clock in the morning. This friend was in his living room on the sofa with the door and windows open. I couldn't believe there were no 'gate' bars."

Paul returned to his reasons for leaving San Francisco.

"One of the reasons I left San Francisco was because I'd known a lot of people who got murdered, mostly drug dealers and stuff like that.

"That was one reason. I'd known another guy, a bully, who was probably about five feet, eight inches and about one hundred and fifty pounds. I saw him get his head blown off.

"I almost got killed one night. I was dancing in this club. I saw a guy come though the door, and I saw buckshot spray. Then I saw the man dancing near me go down. I saw it. I didn't see the other guy actually pull the gun out. But I remember his having a gun, and a boom-boom.

"A young cousin of mine had died in a car accident. His father was speeding and flipped. He had his two-year-old son with him. The boy ended up trapped under the car. His father had a broken arm, and that was it. The father died a few years later.

"I had a lot of family members who got involved in drugs and stuff. I had an uncle who got killed. He was a bus driver and got killed on his bus over some kind of crack deal. I had another cousin get killed over that stuff. His girlfriend killed him.

"Then I had another cousin who killed two people over the stuff. He ended up getting five years. His brother shot some guy in the neck. It didn't kill the guy, just paralyzed him.

"I have another cousin who started getting strung out on the stuff. She had three kids, two-years, three-years, and four-years. She lived in the projects in San Francisco. She'd give the dope dealer the kids for a couple of days until she got the money to get them back. She ended up on a bad trip, taped her kids' mouths, tied them up, and they smothered and died. We found out later she had problems like schizophrenia.

"I have one cousin on my side of the family. His name was Dale. They were in Louisiana. He was an only kid. Both parents died and left him everything. He used all the drugs, used up the house, money, and everything. He ended up getting killed. I had another cousin, found in the San Francisco Hills, beheaded. Those things all led up to my leaving San Francisco, and explain how I ended up in this Program."

We returned to Paul's early experiences in Oregon.

"I had met my son's mother in *****. We were together for two years and then we had a son. Then after about seven years, I decided to move to Eugene and go to school again.

"She'd just had a big promotion. I was arguing, 'He's my son and he's coming with me.' She said, 'No he's not.' I packed all my stuff and right before I left, I went back to see him. He had three dresser drawers full of stuff, so I packed his stuff and just took him with me.

"When I got to *****, that was the first time I experienced people calling me the 'N' word. I'd never had that happen before. In San Francisco, in one neighborhood, there may be a Jewish person, a Korean, Mexicans, black and white. Everything's mixed. I broke a couple of knuckles over the 'N' word, but I did grow out of it. Three days after I was in Eugene, I met my daughters' mother. They're eight and three now."

I asked Paul what the hardest thing about the program was for him.

"I don't think I really ever had a hard time. For the first couple of semesters, it was getting past Ruth. I figured if I could get an 'A' from Ruth, I could make it through. The first time I got a 'C+' from Garry, and then I always got an 'A' from her after that. The hard things were getting good study habits after not being in school for fifteen years, getting though the math, and learning to type.

"My favorite class was 'Ethics.' I liked 'Dual Diagnosis,' but I never knew where I stood with Garry, but I ended up with an 'A'. I liked Toni's classes. I always got an 'A' from Toni because all I had to do was talk and do the work.

"I liked the Forum classes because the class would get heated. A couple of times, I thought they were going to have fistfights."

Paul talked about what he gained out of his Forum.

"I adopted the saying, 'You've got to know what you're going to be getting into.' This was good field experience. I saw what happens in a group setting. I was always waiting for the next class to see what would happen.

"The hard part was seeing some of the people go back to drugs like our friend, *****. I learned a lot about life in those classes by being able to watch people and to be with people.

"That's why I sometimes catch the bus. So I can sit on the bus and see whole lots of things. I can see kids with ADD, the kids with fetal alcohol syndrome. I can pick out a lot of stuff, just sitting back and watching people. I catch myself doing it all the time."

Paul then talked about his interning.

"I've got a group of kids that meets once a week, who got into trouble because of alcohol and drugs. They're in what's called 'Rap' court. It's one of the few in the country. If you complete their program and do whatever the program tells you to do, then you graduate. They will give you your record, and you can actually shred it.

"These kids come for selling drugs, and stealing to get drugs. They come from really dysfunctional families. The parents do drugs, and that's all the kids have ever known. So they just get into trouble, stealing cars and getting 'Minor in Possession' charges. So on Tuesday night, we get together and talk about stuff.

"I also co-facilitate a depression group, which really helps me. You'd be surprised to see people come in, just down. I mean people so debilitated that they can't even talk. All they can do is just sit there and do nothing. My heart goes out to them.

"The course is a twelve-week situation. Each week you teach them about something new: scheduling, how to give compliments, all this kind of stuff. Most of them aren't mandated by the court to come. They come because they've got the *Oregon Health Plan, which may not be around long. So the counselors write grants and try to work around that.

"I sit in on an anxiety group and a discovery group. That's for people who've been mandated. We go over things like thinking errors, and I do motivational interviewing. And I sit in on the relapse prevention groups. So I've learned a whole lot. It's a good fit for me."

I asked Paul where he wanted to be two years from now.

"Working towards a Master's Degree in Science. I'm a junior now. So I've got a lot of stuff that I'll be able to transfer over. I do about twenty-five to thirty hours of CO-OP every week."

I asked him if he was hoping to get his Ph.D.

"As long as the money's coming in. Life experience and all that stuff makes it better for you. So even though I'm forty now, it's what kind of field can I get into? I love being with people.

"I've always been a person who would blurt out everything I felt. I do a lot of thinking before I talk now. I've learned a few things along the way. I'm really happy with it, with myself too."

My last question was what Paul wanted for his kids. He'd brought his little girls to class with him. They were so well-behaved, and their eyes just got bigger and bigger. We all fell in love with them. We weren't able to meet his son, but we knew about him.

"I think it would be great for them to be happy, prosperous, and a respected part of society. I hope they'd follow whatever path they get on and lead a good life without going to jail and without getting on drugs.

"My girls are a lot different with me than they are with their mom. I grew up when you did what your parents said. You didn't talk back. That's the way they are with me. But I didn't get a whole lot of love from my stepfather. I don't think I ever got a hug or kiss from him. So I will always show my kids love.

"I just want them to be loved and be able to love—to be able to give back and not be selfish people who always think about themselves. Even though I'm tough on them, they cool off and are right back in my lap.

"My grandmother made sure we went to church every Sunday, but on Saturday night my mother wouldn't let me go out. That's how I got in trouble. So I figured to myself that I would let my girls go places 'cause if you always tell them no, they'll sneak out.

"I started my son playing baseball at five. Then it was 'all-star.' He plays center field, shortstop, and pitcher. I taught him to play football. He's a middle linebacker, a running back. And he never leaves the game.

"I started talking college at first grade. He'll be going somewhere, as long as I can keep him just floating. I think he'll be back up here in September because he got in trouble at school and got expelled. Some kid had to have some ADD medicine, passed it on to another kid, and passed it to him. He passed it to another kid, and he's on camera. So he got expelled for four months. I'll have him, and these are big years.

"When my son lived with me, he'd get awards for the most hours of reading. I'd make him read for fifteen minutes before he went to bed and document it. Then I'd ask him for reading comprehension and what he read about. I'd make sure he went to homework club. I told him he needed to learn how to do this now, so that when he got out on his own, he'd have good study habits. He'd know how to study the right way. Then he can go wherever he wants and do whatever he needs to do."

We then returned to Paul's plans for the future.

"I'm thinking I'm going to transfer down to Southern Oregon. They have a good Master's Degree program I'm thinking about majoring in psychology. With all the practical work experience, I've had, pretty soon I'll be able to work with the mental health people. I'll be able to work with just about any population. I'll know about drugs and alcohol and whatever else they're going through.

"I want to work in the jails with prisoners. I want to work with them because they'll get out one day and they'll be doing the same stuff. There's a lot of drugs and alcohol in prison. When they come out, they're not going to be able to make much money. The only place they're going to be able to afford is in a drug neighborhood, and the cycle will start again. So I can get with them in prison and teach them some good skills. Then, when they get out, they can do something with it, instead of hanging out with the people they were in jail with. So we'll see."

JOLENE'S STORY

Jan's Apartment, Eugene, Oregon, Spring 2003

Jolene has a big smile and a melodious laugh that lifts my spirits whenever I hear it. She was always willing to help other students. She brought her son to our pizza party. At first I didn't see a resemblance, but then he smiled. It was the same happy smile that Jolene has.

Klutz that I am, I didn't have the recorder on for the first part of the tape, so we will start at another point in her life. Jolene does make reference to previous events and situations in her life that she shared before I remembered to turn on the tape. I think I've presented her story accurately, and we start her memories here.

"My girlfriend had made herself a counseling appointment. At the last minute she decided not to go, so I went. I sat through a whole hour with this guy. He thought I was my friend. I finally said that she decided not to come, but I kept her appointment.

"So I got a little counseling there. He asked me to write a contract about not doing any drugs, which I did, but didn't live up to it. I was still doing everything, just a little of everything, acid, mushrooms, and speed and smoking lots of pot. Later, I got into heavier use, so I did some more counseling with him. I never did stop the drugs and after awhile stopped going."

Jolene talked about her fourth marriage.

"I met my fourth husband when I was about twenty-five or twenty-six. I was working and had to go to welfare for something, so I hitchhiked to the welfare in Spokane. I met him there. He walked up and asked me what I thought about all the VD. I looked at him like he was really strange. This was right after St. Helen's blew, and he was asking, 'You know, volcanic dust.' That was his opener, his pick-up line."

"So I got wrapped up with him. He asked me to go to Texas with him. So my older daughter and I headed for Texas. I didn't know this guy very well, and he was very abusive. He was on the run. He'd escaped from prison. He was an armed robber of drugstores. He hung around with transients and other big-time, heavy criminals. When we got to Texas, we rented this little house. He started bringing home all the street people, so we had this house of about thirty street people.

"By this time I was shooting drugs. He'd hold guns on me. He was very physically abusive. I was in the hospital a few times. At one point he beat the crap out of me and the doctor put me on Valium and painkillers, but it was less than what I was doing anyway. It must have calmed me down enough to get pregnant the second time, and I was out of it most of the time. People had to baby-sit me.

"I remember being alone at the house one time. I answered the door. It was the landlord, and I said that no one else was there, and that I didn't know what's going on. I heard him say to someone. 'Well, where's the little old lady who answered the door?' That was me, and I was still only in my twenties.

"We moved with the weather. In summertime, we were in the Northwest. In the wintertime, we were usually in Texas. We made money by stealing, robbing, and selling drugs on the street. We used to go to concerts and things like that. I'd sell real drugs, and I'd sell bunk drugs.

"My husband was teaching people how to rob drugstores. The Texas police were chasing us. We worked the pipeline for a while and lived in rest areas. The couple we were moving around with was arrested and put in jail. We escaped, went to Austin, and stayed there for awhile."

I asked Jolene about the ages of her children.

"I still only had the one. She'd started kindergarten. I got pregnant. We lived in this trailer that was just rot and bug and cockroach infested. I even had the baby there too. I remember getting up and finding dead cockroaches in her diaper, and fire ants were biting the older one. We moved out of there to a different place.

"Then all the street people started moving in. I got out of that situation because my family was having a family reunion in Oregon, and my folks sent me money to fly home. At that time, the baby was about eight months old.

"My husband made it really miserable the whole night before I left. I was sitting in the corner while he badmouthed me and threatened me. He'd spent it all. He did get someone else to give me the money to fly home. So I came home to The Dalles with the two kids and did not go back.

"I was going to go back, but then I finally broke down and told my folks how it really was. I wasn't getting along with my folks. My mother gave me two weeks to get out of her house, and so I did. I got a little apartment in The Dalles for the three of us and started getting some counseling again. I slowed down on the drugs some, but not a whole lot. I wasn't shooting drugs at that time.

"I hooked up with another guy. I became pregnant for the third time. That was my son.

"By then my fourth husband was on the way to Oregon. I was scared to death because I'd made the step of leaving. I tried to get some mental health help, but for some reason they didn't think I needed it. So I hooked up with another guy. I stay married to this last one for five years. We didn't live together for the whole five years. We know each other from high school and were using and shooting drugs.

Jolene started to tell how she began recovery.

"My second daughter was four, and I was working at a pizza place. I'd worked my way up to being the night manager. I met this lady who was in A.A., and she talked a lot about A.A. I remember going on vacation with my husband, and we shot a whole lot of drugs.

"In the meantime, my fourth husband had been caught robbing another drugstore. He was back in prison. He called me one time and told me he was in A.A. in prison. I was sitting on top of the steps. I couldn't even see the bottom of the steps.

"I started losing control of my body. I'd wake up, and I'd pooped myself. I started not having control over some of those things.

"So I woke up one day and called this lady from work. I told her, that I didn't drink much, but when I drink, I drink to excess and I know that I'm a drug addict and don't know anything about recovery. So she came over and the first thing she did was make me go tell everyone. That was about the hardest thing I ever did. I went to my job and told my boss I needed to go to treatment.

"By this time I was really closet using, but I could be in a hot kitchen, wearing long-sleeved sweaters to cover the tracks. I'd even sneak out during work and go shoot in the parking lot.

"I was doing things like that, and the drug use was so bad that I was contemplating leaving the kids and going back to the street. My habits were getting harder and harder to pay for. Anyway, she made me go tell my folks. My second husband and his new wife came over. They were both in A.A.

"I was locked in my parents' basement, and they all sat with me all night. Neighbors took care of the kids. The next day, the lady, my friend, and my mother drove me to a detox in Pendleton.

"The Pendleton detox didn't want me because I was coming off drugs and not alcohol. They sent me upstairs to the drug unit, and I came off of drugs up there. I was there for maybe four days.

"Then they told me my insurance wasn't good enough, so they sent me farther east to Ontario, Oregon, for this twenty-eight day program, and I stayed there for twenty-eight days. Of course, I got into a relationship while I was there. Besides drugs, I'm addicted to relationships. I'm looking for something in a man. I don't know what, but I never did find it.

"I was serious about what I was doing, but I was smoking pot in the treatment center. I came home and stayed clean, not for very long. I remember going up to get my thirty-day medallion at A.A., stoned on pot.

"About that time, my first husband had been killed. There was a lot of love there, but that's just the way things were. So he was killed, and I was grieving. I ended up smoking pot. I never did go back to the speed. I did continue to smoke pot and drink. I quit going to A.A.

"So this guy from treatment and I used for a couple of years. Then he started getting in to the white dope, speed, and coke pretty bad and started stealing, lying, and everything. I finally just called it quits and told him he had to leave or quit using. So he left. I went back to A.A., helped start a group in The Dalles, and my recovery started.

"That's when I was pretty messed up. I had three kids One was a baby, one was probably six, and the other one in her early teens. So I had three kids as a single parent working nights, swing shift. I got real heavy into recovery, went to ninety meetings in ninety days, and got really involved.

"My oldest decided that it was time that I came back and started being a parent because she was doing all the parenting. She would be the parent and keep the kids while I worked at night. She threatened to go live with her dad if I didn't change things. I tried to get my job to change schedules, but that didn't happen, so I quit my job and went on welfare.

"At that time, welfare started having things like the jobs program. It was called 'life skills' back them. It was my first year in recovery; I started counseling with the director of this program. I graduated out of that and I went on to get an Associate's Degree. This director went into private practice, but she continued to counsel me for eight years for free.

"We went through quite a lot of issues. I had never dealt with any of the abuse or the abortion, and I never dealt with the time when I lost the child between the two girls. I always thought that because of the abortion, God wasn't going to let me have this man. I was very angry with God.

"I didn't have any kind of relationship with my family. Even with my son's dad, I was the bitch because I threw him out. I was trying to get my life together. You know, at least he worked. I didn't have a relationship with my family for about three years. Then things started changing with them.

"My son and my second daughter were going to meetings with me because I didn't have anyone to watch them. So they grew up in recovery, especially my son. My middle child got a little bit of both. I'm surprised my oldest turned out as well as she did. She went through everything. So I stayed clean for six-and-a-half years, got an Associate's Degree in general studies, and was in a lot of counseling.

"I got a job working at a boy's residential home. I did that for about a year and a half. Now it's more of a day treatment and proctor care at night. During that change we were all laid off. They had trained me to be an advanced proctor care person, but I got real sick and never went into it. My second daughter started her addiction, so it wasn't a good idea to bring in more troubled kids when I had one of my own.

"When I was six-and-a-half years clean, I was doing a stretch with Americorps and I was doing really well. I hooked up with this guy. It never fails. He was in recovery, but started drinking. I remember asking a friend of mine who had two years sobriety to come over and be with me because he was drinking. She came over and started drinking with him.

"I was sponsoring a lot of people in A.A. I was big on the A.A. and N.A. board, but I wasn't happy. I told myself I was never an alcoholic. I can drink. So I drank and I went through this big self-destructive thing and started cutting on myself. I was in my thirties. I had to go back to counseling. It was like starting all over.

"While I went through this, I had some bad experiences. My sponsor started drinking at the time and told everybody that I gave her the alcohol, so nobody in A.A. was really happy with me. I never really went back to those particular meetings.

"My own relapse lasted for only two months. It wasn't every day drinking. I don't remember getting drunk. I was so down on myself for blowing it that I got myself back together again and started working. Had a year of this guy's drinking and finally kicked him out. So I was back in recovery, but I was doing it alone. I went to an A.A. meeting once in a while, but really just disconnected.

"My oldest had moved out and had a family of her own. My second daughter started using. When my son was about ten and she was about fourteen, she was beating him up while I was working. He told his dad, and I let him go live with his dad. It's the hardest thing I ever had to do. Shortly after that, she was put in the Oregon Youth Authority and removed from the home too.

"So all of a sudden, I'm home alone. I went through a whole year of severe depression. My daughter was in and out of different treatment centers. She ran away from two. They finally put her in a lock-up one.

"I got real co-dependent with her. She was seventeen. She came home in August. My son came back, and so, after a year of not having any kids, I had two kids, and I just wasn't doing very well. When the kids were gone for that year, I went through an empty-nest period, lots of crying and 'Woe is me,' and then they were back all of a sudden.

"I worked as a cook for Head Start. When my daughter came home, she stayed clean for a short while. At the very end of August, she started using again. In December, she and some other girls did a burglary. She had just gotten off probation, out of the Oregon Youth Authority, and then got caught doing that.

"I decided that I needed to do something. I just couldn't continue to be miserable in my co-dependency with her. She wasn't ready, so I made the decision to go to school.

"I had a high school friend in Eugene, and she said for me to come on down here. So the kids and I moved down here. I did a thing with HUD—section, eight—a self-sufficiency program for five years and earned about $5000 to go back to school.

"I moved down here probably in February. My daughter was already using with her friends. I put her back in an outpatient treatment, and then she went to a residential program in Corvallis.

"I started school in the summertime. I did the women's program. I still wasn't sure. I'd always wanted to do drug and alcohol counseling, but I was so tired of being around drug and alcohol people. So I did the women's program and all the testing came up teaching, counseling, or something peoplewise.

"I didn't want to drag it out like my first Associate's Degree and just end up with a general Associate's. So I did our Program and graduated. I'm still working in the field. I'm still not going to a lot of meetings. I'm still not reaching out, but I am staying clean and sober. I guess I just don't have the urge any more.

"I'm an example for the clients, and so life is okay. There are still things I need to change. I'm still dealing with my daughter's addiction. She's actually on her way home today. She's in and out. She's not really living with me. I allow her to bring her stuff here.

"Last summer, she took my bank card, went to the bank, and took all my money, about three hundred dollars. She stole a car. The guy got his car back, but she hasn't lived with me since.

"On Christmas Eve, she called me and said 'Mom, can I come home or do I have to sleep on a bench?' She'd been prostituting, stealing, and robbing. I cleaned her up. She's starting to get the drug psychosis. She's hearing things and is paranoid. I'm hoping it's not going to be a permanent thing. It's really scaring her, but as soon as she starts feeling better, she starts using again.

"I'm still dealing with her addictions, but I'm doing better. I can set boundaries with her now. I'm not so co-dependent, even though it hurts my heart. I guess I just got to the point where I know that I can't do anything about it. The more I try to talk to her about it, the worse it gets. Every time I make a suggestion, she blames me and says I'm why she uses. So I try not to talk to her about it too much."

We talked about Jolene's opinions and experiences in the CDCT Program.

"I liked all the teachers. 'Forum' was okay. I didn't mind the work. I did okay. I think the hardest part for me was going through the Program while I was still fighting the co-dependency of my daughter's addictions.

"I think the Program taught me a lot about how to deal with her addiction. There were a couple of times when I wondered why I was doing this—living on just grant money. I had both kids, so we were living very poor.

"I see a lot of dual diagnosis. That was the class I had the worst time in. Not so much that it was so hard for me, but the project they gave us was a group thing. My group just didn't function very well. We got an okay grade, but I think there were a lot of personality conflicts."

I asked Jolene about her work and if she was worried about being let go because of the entire budget cuts in social and other services.

"Not so much me. I'm on the graveyard shift that nobody wants. I do have some one-on-one, but most of the time the women are sleeping. I connect with their babies during the graveyard shift because a lot of the babies are addicted, so they're up all night.

"We have this one little guy. He's not so much addicted to the drug his mom was doing, but his mom is schizophrenic and takes lithium and haldol, so the baby was withdrawing from that too. He used to have tremors and shakes, but he's much better now. He has a lot of personality. He's a cute little guy.

"I've been looking more into dual diagnosis because I'm watching my own daughter starting some psychosis stuff. I worry about how some of the patients are going to survive if there are more cuts."

For my last question, I asked Jolene if she thought she might go back to school.

"Well, I've got this Associate's Degree, but you look in the paper now, and they want a Bachelor's or a Master's. So I've been thinking about it. For some reason, the University of Oregon scares me, but there are other colleges around here. So I think I might. I'm going to have to pick a college, take them all my transcripts, and see."

JOANIE'S STORY

Jan's Apartment, Eugene, Oregon, Spring 2003

Joanie and I met at an intensive grief seminar in August before school actually started. One of the exercises was letting each other put wet mask-making paper on each other's face. When we were finished and removed the masks, we designed our masks to represent significant events or people in our lives. We had fun and gained insights into our own grief and traumas as well as each other's. I felt that I really knew Joanie and was happy to see her in our first Forum.

As the year progressed, I felt very close to Joanie. She was a single mom with one son. She brought him to our pizza party just before graduation, and he charmed everyone.

I first asked Joanie about her childhood, her family, and early schooling.

"There are six and I'm second to the youngest, five girls and one boy. From very early on, I remember alcohol and alcoholism playing a part in my life. Around four or five, I became aware of my grandfather's active alcoholism. Shortly after that, I became aware of my dad's drinking. I don't know if it was active alcoholism at that point, but I was aware of it.

"I remember when his drinking became very apparent. I specifically remember being embarrassed when I had cousins over from the 'good' side of the family. They were involved in their church and just very stable normal families.

"My first four years of school were great, including kindergarten. I was born on the coast in North Bend, Oregon. In the summer before fourth grade, we moved to Eugene. The business was expanding. We were opening up a store in Eugene. That's when I became acutely aware of my dad's drinking.

"Starting the business was really tough and took a toll on the family. These were different dynamics. This wasn't something I saw in the other kids' families. So there was a tough adjustment in the fourth grade: new city, the move, new kids, and being the new kid in the classroom.

"It was an awkward age for me going from a smaller town, knowing all the kids, being a part of and a leader in the classroom, to being the new kid on the block. This was along with the turmoil that was going on in my family. From fourth grade on, I was acutely aware of my dad's drinking.

"I had a hard time adjusting. Kids could be really cruel. I'd never been the underdog or the brunt of the joke. I'd always been the one to take the side of the underdog and to stick up for someone else who was being picked on. I was singled out, and everything was magnified during that year. I remember talking to the school counselor and just crying my eyes out. Looking back now, a lot of that was probably hugely influenced by what was going on at home.

"My father owned a retail clothing company. The business got started, settled in, and established a clientele. It got to a point where it looked as if the business was going to make it. The stress was gone, but, of course, my father's drinking continued.

"I wasn't in any trouble in the rest of my grade school years. I just remember my father was really strict. Dad made the rules. What he said went. My mother and dad were both strict, but it was probably as much a result of his dominance in the power scheme in the house as anything.

"There were a lot of things I wasn't allowed to do that other kids of my age were. In fifth grade the popular girls organized a rally for the boys' sports. At that time, I was always on and off. That was really difficult because one day I was their friend and the next one I wasn't. I usually didn't know where I stood. It was great when I was a part of the group and horrendous when I wasn't.

"At the time of the rally, I was allowed to be a part of the group. I wanted to be in on the rally, but of course my father said I couldn't because I was too young. That was another way I became aware of being different from the other kids. It didn't help.

"At that age, we want to be a part of or equal to the other kids. The more we could blend in the better. I was still trying to blend in and sometimes with no difference in any behavior on my part, but the ebb and flow of the other girls' feelings decided whether I was 'in.' That continued in fourth, fifth, and sixth grades.

"The first time I drank was probably the summer between sixth and seventh grade. At the time, I didn't realize the significance of it, but I drank to a complete annihilation blackout and got sick. I was with a friend's family on the beach.

"We were on the beach drinking. I do remember bits and pieces of having to crawl at some point to get where we were going. I don't remember being aware of it at the time, but I was painfully aware of it the next morning.

"I don't know if I actively remembered getting sick, but I knew I had been because all the bedding had to be stripped. I was feeling horrible, sick, and still intoxicated. I remember worrying about my parents and if they would find out. They had to have known. There's no way they couldn't have known. This was my first experience with alcohol. From the very first time, I drank to blackout. So that's an indication of my story.

"I don't remember drinking being a regular part of my activities at that point, but shortly after that, I started smoking marijuana. I think that was very early on. I became a daily smoker. That continued for years and years. That was constant until I got into recovery at thirty.

"The only time I remember not smoking pot was when I'd run out, and I remember those times as being miserable. I didn't want to do anything until I had some marijuana. I just wanted to stay in bed and cover my head until I had some more.

"As I got older, I think the drinking escalated. What happened to me when I did drink, was not having any control once I started. No matter what my intentions were, I'd think that I wasn't going to drink much that night. I'd just have a few, but once I had the first two or three, I just lost track of EVERYTHING.

"The drinking to blackout was actually a horrendous experience at the time. Although I think it was easy to keep moving and minimize the shame and guilt that I know I felt. After I was old enough to drink legally, there was a bunch of us who would go out almost every night. It was such a consistent pattern. I was often the driver, but with the grace of God, I definitely felt I was carried through many situations. I was really blessed and very fortunate with my drinking and driving.

"But it became a pattern. I remember getting my girl friends home. After I dropped the last one off, I could never remember getting myself home. Every morning, I called the girls and asked what happened and how I seemed to them. They would say I seemed fine. I asked if I seemed really drunk, or if I was falling down drunk. Then they would assure me that it seemed like I was just having fun.

"Fun! I just didn't get it. There would be a magical cut-off point where I just went on autopilot. I think I was able to push it in the back of my mind. It really bothered me. It was scary. I just continued functioning and couldn't remember it later.

"At the time I was working. Of course, I was pretty flaky. I avoided responsibility and getting to work on time. My partying was the priority. I fit work in when I could.

"There was a middle period before going back to work for my father's company when I was doing 'waitressing.' Probably the longest I ever held a waitressing job was four to six months."

I asked Joanie if she and those friends were still in contact with each other.

"We all eventually went our own ways. I've seen one of them a couple of times recently. Since I started in the Program and working in the field, I've actually seen cases of people I know and where they've ended up.

"There's this section in the A.A. big book where the people say they quit just in time. That's my story. I ran into this girlfriend who was the friend that I was the most consistent with and remained friends with the longest.

"We were each other's party buddies. It's really sad seeing the toll that the disease has taken on her. How fortunate I've been. How different and how widely separated the roads are, once you either make that turn to the right or to the left. It just amazes me.

"Since working in the field, I've gotten the sense of how lucky I am. I quit in the nick of time. People tell me that I never shot drugs. I was a high *bottom drunk, but for me, my bottom was the bottom. It was spiritual, emotional, moral, and all those things."

Joanie talked about her experiences with drinking and driving.

"I never did get jail time as a result of my drinking or drugging which astonishes me. I remembered getting stopped many time. There were many times when I was stopped when I should have been ticketed, but I either talked my way out of it, or they knew my father.

"This is back in the time when you could still get away with that. Or if you were a young girl, and they thought you were cute. If I were still drinking and doing any of those things, I'm sure I'd be taken straight to jail.

"There was one time when one guy pulled me out of a ditch. This is the big blackout story that started leading to my recovery even though it didn't happen right away. It took a few years. The cop had been in the Marine Corps with my uncles. Instead of taking me in, he called my aunt. This was at, oh my God, three in the morning.

"There was another time that I got pulled over because my taillights were out. I should have gone in that time too. We'd been smoking in the car, so it smelled like pot, and we were drinking. I was intoxicated, but I pulled myself together when the officer walked up to the car, I think that was the one who had been in the state police force with my other uncle. I think there's a lot that kept me from being arrested. That may be good or bad.

"I feel really fortunate that I never hurt someone else or myself. It astounds me with doing this much drinking and drugging and partying. About this time I got involved with cocaine, and that definitely was the beginning of the end for me as far as leading to my bottom. Cocaine was custom-made for someone like me. From the first time I did it, I loved it. I wanted more and couldn't get enough."

Joanie returned to the big blackout story.

"I remember that every time I went out, I was thinking that I just might meet 'him.' I think I was always on the search for 'him.' I never did find 'him.' There was one night in particular. I'd gone out by myself. The bar called last call. It was really standard for me to double up for last call. I think I ordered two, double Black Russians. I probably slammed those down in a ten- or-twenty-minute period.

"I remember this guy coming up to the bar. I won't call him a friend, just an acquaintance. He dealt with cocaine, and I remember getting cocaine from him. I don't even know if I liked him all that much as a person. He ordered more Black Russians for me. I remember thinking he was involved in the rest of what happened. This was one of the most profound experiences of my life.

"I think I remember being on a road somewhere out in the ***** area. And someone was with me in my father's truck. The next thing I knew I was in a police car between three, four, or maybe five in the morning. The police officer was telling me my aunt would come to pick me up.

"I had no idea where I'd been. I had my father's vehicle, and my parents were out of town. I remember talking to the police officer. I was trying to find out where I'd been without letting him know that I had no clue. I knew someone was with me. Now I was trying to find out where the truck was. It was in ***** in a ditch. I remember saying something to the officer about *****, and he said that I wasn't in *****. I was in *****.

"What had happened was that there was a private road. I'd run though the gate. I dragged this tree stump about a hundred yards, pulled the fence down, and ended up in a ditch. I told the officer, someone was with me and asked where was the other person? They told me there was no other person. I was by myself. Then I panicked again. What happened to me?

"The police officer said that I was very fortunate because if I hadn't gone into the ditch, I would have ended up on a railroad track. So there I would have sat in my father's car on the track waiting for the early morning train to come though. That was when I started getting really scared of my drinking.

"It took a few more years before recovery. My family tried an intervention when I was about twenty-six or twenty-seven. That was a time when I got into more of a long time relationship—my first, long time, adult relationship. We were living together and talking about getting married. Eventually we become engaged even though I knew in my heart that I didn't want to marry this person. But I'd thought for a while that I had found 'him.' So I didn't have to go to the bars and drink to blackout anymore to find him. So the bar drinking and all that stuff stopped. But we started doing cocaine on a more consistent basis. He took to the cocaine as much as I did.

"That's when the family became involved. I had a brother who had been in rehab a few times and had been in and out of recovery. He had gotten me cocaine, and I had gotten him cocaine. After one of his trips to rehab, he came back and was going to 'fix' me. This was when they attempted the intervention.

"Some of the confrontations weren't valid for me because one of them was coming from a sister who'd had me get her cocaine just two weeks before. Another was coming from a brother who had just gotten me cocaine. So it all had very little validity for me.

"My father was still drinking. I think he had gone through his first rehab by then. I think he's been through treatment four or five times now at all the major treatment centers. He still struggles with active alcoholism.

"The intervention didn't take. When I turned thirty, I was ready. In fact, it was on my thirtieth birthday. My relationship had split up. I was a Marilyn Monroe fan, and I was living in this little studio apartment in this big house. I was paying about $150 a month and probably borrowing to pay the rent because I was doing a lot of cocaine.

"I remember sitting there, looking at my posters of Marilyn, and thinking that I was doing cocaine by myself because I preferred to do it that way. It was no longer fun or a social activity because I got so 'tweaked out.' There are a lot of meth users who use that term now, but when I say 'tweaked out,' I'm referring to cocaine.

"I didn't like meth. Meth was below me, you know, as if cocaine was less harmful. I remember looking at Marilyn and thinking that I wasn't going to live to be thirty-six. That's when she died. I wouldn't make it if I kept this up.

"No matter how much cocaine I had, I craved it, wanted it more than even the people who were dealing. Even they could stop and get to the point where they'd had enough and go to sleep. If I'd had an endless supply, I would have killed myself. The only thing that stopped me was that I had limited access and limited finances. I always wanted more.

"I had one experience where I did it right after I had an abortion. Looking back, I can see that was really crazy. Something electrical in my heart clicked. My heart was doing some funny things, and it was stuck. Then it was jumping and going. It got into a weird rhythm like 'doo, doo, doo, and doo.'

"That's what it did and I thought, 'Oh my God is this it? Am I going to die?' I remember going to the bathroom and passing a huge blood clot. I got my heart settled down and back to a normal rhythm. I went back into the living room and continued doing cocaine. That was probably midway in my cocaine experience. So that wasn't even at the peak of my use. But I knew, that finding the dose that would satisfy me, would be the dose that killed me."

Joanie and I stopped to relax and get some cookies and coffee. We talked about her son's placement in school and how traumatic his first one had been for him. She was scouting out other programs for him. Then we resumed discussing her long trip to real recovery.

"So at thirty, I got into recovery. It took me awhile to get into a treatment center. I had six months of being clean and sober. I was living in a recovery home in California. Then I met this guy who I knew wasn't 'him,' but he was close enough. I met him at six months, and within three weeks, I was drinking again.

"So I was on a run for a while. I didn't do a lot of cocaine. I would have, but I couldn't get it. I was just back into drinking and that was bad enough. I was doing whatever coke I could do. Then I remember dragging myself back to my mom's in San Diego.

"I was so sick. I was pregnant and had a kidney and a bladder infection. I had tried to quit on my own. I went in and out. I'd get thirty days and then go out. I did thirty days, sixty days, or ninety days and went back out.

"Of course none of it was 'my fault.' I could see that the big one was coming. I was doing a lot of drugs back and forth across the Coronado Bridge, and I just knew something bad was going to happen. I had a fender bender with my mom's car. And some other things happened.

"Then I decided I'd had enough. I couldn't do it anymore; I didn't want to do it. Oddly enough, that was the first day I saw a psychiatrist and talked to him about my depression. I started getting some medication for depression from him. That was my first real day of sobriety. I have remained clean and sober ever since.

"I'm a very good example of dual diagnosis. My interests in dual diagnosis are a result of that. I love doing dual diagnosis groups. That's my thing, and that's my forte. I was in a dual diagnosis group for many years, and I didn't want to move on."

I asked Joanie what made her return to Eugene.

"Family. My father was ill, and I had my son. I was in recovery. Thank goodness for that. He was premature—born at twenty-eight weeks. My father had a minor stroke with a seventy-percent blockage, and if it went, he would go too.

"I would rather have stayed in San Diego because I know some of the family dynamics that would come. As much as I love my family, I felt that without my son, I would have stayed in San Diego.

"But taking my son into consideration and my parents getting older and wanting my son to know the only grandparents who were involved in his life, we moved back when he was a year old. We've been here ever since. He's thriving, and I'm still trudging the road to happy destiny."

The tape became garbled at this point so I have to fill in the rest from my memory. Joanie was interning and working at a family clinic and worrying a little about keeping a job because there were so many cuts in the social services.

Joanie thinks about going to school, but hasn't decided yet. She liked the Program, the people she met there, and everything she learned. Her son is her first priority, and her future decisions will revolve around him for several years.

ANGIE'S STORY

Angie's Office, ***** Facility, Eugene, Oregon, Spring 2003

Angie was another very quiet person. We all took a good look at her when we found out that she'd received a perfect score on one of Garry's tests. That was hard to do. I was able to work with her on our video project and a group treatment program for clients suffering from depression in conjunction with alcoholism or drug addiction. We worked hard on both projects and had fun doing them.

I first asked Angie about her childhood.

"When I was in 'utero,' my father was in jail so alcohol was a part of our family. He got out of jail before I was born and actually raised me for my first two years. He didn't drink during that time. Growing up, I remember he did drink, but it never stood out. I never noticed it. He just always had a beer or something around.

"So I didn't really know much of anything about it until my mom was going to kick him out. That's when I actually realized what was going on. I was about eight or nine. He stopped drinking and didn't drink again ever until they got divorced when I was about twenty-three. So it worked. She gave him the choice, and he chose not to drink anymore. But when they split up, of course, he chose to drink some, but that was about it.

"He doesn't get out of control or anything, so I don't know if he's an alcoholic or not. He was able to just quit. If he wants to, he drinks. If he doesn't, he doesn't. He controls it. I'm not sure what his addiction level would be. Abuse, probably, since it's been so many years, but I don't know if it's actual addiction or not. It was always kept from us though."

Angie talked a little about her school experience and her alcohol consumption during that time.

"I always liked school, even in middle school. I loved high school. I didn't do a lot with alcohol. I had a moment in high school where I almost got kicked out, but I didn't. I went to outpatient treatment, just like where I work now. I graduated and was completely drug and alcohol free, except for cigarettes.

"After I graduated from high school, I took a lot of time off. Then I worked for a long, long time. I almost got stuck in that—just going to work nine to five, hard labor mode. I hurt my wrist really bad and my back and finger. Got the fingers caught in a lathe processor where I worked. So I decided that physical labor wasn't really up my alley, so I went back to college."

Angie talked about her experiences with alcohol and her relationships.

"About the time, I was twenty-four, I met a guy who was in the bar scene—a musician type. I would go and watch him and not drink. Then the music got boring because I heard the same thing night after night. So I did drink a little bit, but never out of control. I never had to drink. It was more like, 'Okay, I'm here, so I'll drink.' Sometimes I wouldn't drink at all. I'd just hang out and sometimes drink a little. Sometimes I'd feel it, for sure, but never to the point where I was sick or drinking and driving. I never drove home. Never out of control.

"When I broke up with him, there was no reason to go back to drinking. If it's a special occasion like New Year's Eve, and I'm in Reno and Los Vegas, I'll have a glass of champagne or one mixed drink. Other than that, it's not even a part of my life. Maybe once a year, but it's never been important to me. It was really easy not to do it anymore.

"I really have had no experience with drugs other than nicotine and my coffee addiction, which is bad. Not the nicotine any more. I quit smoking, but I can't do without my caffeine. I tried once, but I had to take a bunch of aspirin. I was miserable, so now I'm back on the caffeine again."

Angie has not yet married, but she talked about another long-term relationship.

"He was—what's that disorder? It wasn't antisocial, but borderline, yeah, borderline. I was with him for two years, and it was crazy. It was frustrating, but I think I learned a lot from it, especially working in this field. The patience I had to have to deal with this guy and the strategies I had to use just to get him back down to reality have really been useful.

"I was with him for two years. We didn't drink or anything in this relationship. That was the one before this. I don't know why I didn't drink. He made me want to drink—if anything could. It was healthy in that way, but not healthy in another. It was just constant arguing."

We then talked about her impressions and experiences in the Program.

"I started in ***** and just took basic math and stuff. When I transferred over here, I realized I could do the math and writing WITH a Program. I was looking at all the different things, and picked up the Chemical Dependency information, and ***** came over and said, 'Boy, you should get into that Program. It's really good.'

"I remembered a report I wrote in the seventh grade about cocaine. I've always been interested in drugs and alcohol. So he was talking about all these cool teachers and about what a wonderful experience this was. So that, the fact that I've always been interested in it, plus it was achievable influenced my decision. So I thought, 'Okay, might as well.' So I did, and I really liked the Program.

"It wasn't what I expected even though ***** told me what I should expect. I almost left the Program two or three times—once in the very beginning. Then I was cool for awhile, but when we had to start doing videotaping and role-playing and doing things in front of the class, I was ready to leave again. Now I do those things all the time. And it's a lot easier to deal with clients instead of peers because the peers are critiquing you. They know what to look for and what you're doing and not doing. It's a lot harder than with clients.

"I originally wanted to work with adults. Then I realized I didn't have the patience for that. I'm not sure why. I just kept going back and forth. I didn't want to work with teenagers. That was too hard, but as soon as I started my internship with teens, I loved it.

"I love working with the teenagers because they're so unpredictable. They're like little sponges. They want an adult to ask them how they are because a lot of them aren't getting that anywhere else. When they're sick, they want me to see if they have a temperature because there's no one else.

"It seems that I have a lot to offer teenagers. I still remember being a teenager and can identify with them. For some reason, they can identify with me too. They're cool clients to work with.

"I'm doing role playing, video taping, and finding my style. I guess I'm still looking, but I'm getting settled in. It's easy to put information in my head and memorize it. That was never a problem. The problem was turning it into my style and applying everything I had learned in my relationship with a client. That was hard."

Angie and I discussed her job and the positive and negative things abut it.

"The hardest part? It's really hard to say. When something goes wrong—and I know I could do something with most kids if I could just get them in here. But for some, I can make phone calls to parents and parole officers, but the clients don't show up. That's the hardest part. Once they're here, I know I have a chance. Something's going to click.

Even if they don't use it right away, someday they will. We're planting all the seeds. We're giving them all the tools.

"Knowing that there's a kid that I could plant something in: a thought, an idea, a fact, something, but I can't get him here. I know he needs to be here and could benefit from being here. At least showing up would get him out of legal consequences. I'm thinking 'Man, he's choosing legal consequences. He must really be in a bad way.' That's hard.

"It's a stressful job, but I'm a well-organized person so the paper work doesn't bother me. It's just about being where I'm supposed to be.

"Once here, I'm fine and can do the paperwork. The job is stressful because I never know what I'm going to hear or have to deal with. But it's something that always gets dealt with. So I try not to stress out too much about it."

Angie talked a little bit about her health. She'd been sick since February with really bad headaches. And the doctors were still trying to find out why.

"In the two years that I've been here, I've only missed one day of work. I felt bad about missing that day, but I was really sick, and my headache medicine wasn't working."

We talked about all the cuts in Social Services and what she would do if her job were eliminated.

"I have no idea. I'm open to just about anything. I have a back-up plan somewhere in my head. Not an actual, 'What steps will I take, but what direction will I go?' If it happens, then I'll formulate the steps. I'll still be doing this job if budgets and everything allows.

"If not, I have two weeks of paid vacation and two weeks of sick leave saved up. I want to do this. That's my goal—to just keep on going. I like being settled in a job. The cool thing about being settled in this job is that it's never boring. So I'll still be doing this in three or five years if I can.

"If not, I'd like to have just a regular physical job for a year. There's no stress to that. My body works harder, but there's no mental stress. I'll go back to school eventually. I'm not sure what for, but it's an option. If I do, it will be about young kids, but I don't know why. School hasn't been something I've totally dismissed. In fact, I've even considered doing something with disabled or handicapped kids, but that's on the back burner."

Angie continued to talk about her work and the strategies she utilizes in this work. I specifically asked her if she'd used the treatment plan we'd worked on together.

"I've actually got it, and I refer to it. Almost half of our kids are dual diagnosis. That's nice because even though I can't diagnose, I can recognize and send them to the right person and place.

"I have anxiety about doing groups, which is no secret to anyone. I get any information I can get my hands on. I have notebook after notebook, just full of notes and handouts. I get catalogs where I can order videos, activities, plans, and books.

"I've done all the groups that we have: process, psycho-educational, and recreation. My groups are the educational groups, the psycho-education groups because I do it well. Less of the 'How do you feel today?' processing groups. I can do them, but if I go into a group with a curriculum, I'm going to tell them everything I know about alcohol.

"I can teach the kids alcohol education so the psycho-education groups are mine because my supervisors think I'm good at it. I've become more comfortable because of this. I go in and do it. It's not just about how it makes them feel because most of the kids don't know what alcohol and drugs do to them physically. So if you add that to a processing group and a recreation group, it's a complete package."

For my final question, I asked Angie if she had any last thoughts.

"I do. I really like what I do, and that's important. My own experiences with drugs and alcohol have been somewhat limited, but it's always been around me in some way. I've gained experience. Being around an alcoholic is another tool to use in this field. I feel that it's at least forty percent experience, not just drug and alcohol experience, but life experience.

"It's cool. I like it. I even like the bad days because it's never a totally bad day. Something good comes out of every day that I've been here.

"It's never a bust. It was a good choice so I'll be here until the place shuts down. Worst-case scenario? If the place would go down, I'm prepared for that. But I'll stay here for as long as I can, for sure. There are those days when even though it's not a bust, I'm really tired.

"But overall, it really isn't like work. Sometimes I wonder that I get paid for this. Sometimes, I think, 'I don't get paid for THIS, but that's maybe like fifteen minutes out of a week. The rest of the time, I'm like 'Yea!' It's a great feeling."

JAN'S STORY

Jan's House, Florence Oregon, Spring 2005

"When I first decided to write this book, I thought I could just narrate the stories my classmates told me and stay aloof from the secrets they revealed. However, it soon became clear that if I expected my classmates to delve deep into their past and admit some horrendous problems and actions, I had to come clean too.

"So here is my story—all seventy-one years of it. I was born in Chicago, Illinois, on Thanksgiving Day, November 30, 1933. My favorite family story is about how my mother prepared Thanksgiving dinner, washed the dishes, and then departed for the hospital to have me at five minutes before ten. At home were my older sister, nine and older brother, not yet two.

"When I was three, we moved to a small village outside Chicago, Illinois, in what was probably one of the first subdivisions. It was all prairies, and the developer would come once a week to take the housewives into a bigger town for grocery shopping.

"Although I don't remember a lot, I do remember some things about the Depression in those years before World War II. We ate a lot of oatmeal. Our electricity was cut off. On Thanksgiving, we received a food basket. I thought it was for my birthday.

"About that time, I noticed that sometimes I didn't like to be around the daddy I adored. I hate to admit it, but he was an alcoholic. Yet, I loved him very much, and it hurts to say that he was an alcoholic. When he was sober, he was witty, charming, and interested in us. He taught me many things, which I still remember today. He encouraged me to go to college and insisted I finish my Master's Degree so that I could still live at home to save money.

"My dad got a good job as police chief, and my brother and I were thrilled when he let us ride in the squad car. Unfortunately, my dad was involved in a drunken driving accident involving a death. Although he was acquitted, he lost his job. That didn't stop him from drinking, but, as far as I know, he didn't drive again until I was in college. We never talked about this. As in most families, who deal with addiction, secrets were kept. My younger sister was born at home at night while a blizzard raged outside.

"In December 1940, my dad got a good job at a defense plant in Indiana. We sold our village house and purchased one on the north side of the city. My younger brother was born in 1941. My aunt who had heart trouble lived with us. And later my granddad, a widower and a pharmacist, moved in too. My dad kept drinking, but he held onto that job until the war was over. Then he worked for the Veterans Administration until he retired.

"Moving to Indiana was traumatic for me. I moved from a school where most students were poor to a school where many of the students came from affluent families. I had a hard time making friends, and, except for ***** who lived behind us, I was pretty lonely. In the spring, I came down with rheumatic fever and missed the last weeks of school. That summer I became involved with the neighborhood pedophile.

"This neighbor even bought me a bicycle. About that time, I was suppressing all of my guilt and misery, but I finally had the courage to tell him. 'No, it's wrong and I'm not going to do anything like that anymore.'

"He had the nerve to ask my mother what he had done to make me avoid him. I didn't tell anyone, and when the bike that he'd bought me was stolen, I was glad, but I never let on.

"That secret festered and festered until that neighbor started showing an interest in my younger sister. I told my mother then. That was the bravest thing I've ever done in my life. My mother was shocked and dismayed, but she held me, talked to me, and told me it wasn't my fault. However, we couldn't tell my dad or my granddad because they would do something horrible to that neighbor. In those days no one told!

"My mother felt so guilty because she had trusted the neighbor, and even after I was grown, would tell me how sorry she was that she had let that happen to me. I don't know who in my family knew. I imagine my older sister did, but I don't know of anyone else for sure. I hate writing all of this.

"That neighbor is long since dead, but I wonder now how many other young girls he seduced with attention and gifts in the guise of a good neighbor who liked little girls. I know of at least three. No one noticed that my brother was never welcome on any of our excursions.

"I also wonder how many neighbors knew and didn't tell my mother. I've only told a few people about this, but I still feel guilty when people talk about pedophilia, even though I was the child, and he was the master seducer. This was another secret, which should have been let out, and the culprit punished and put where no other little girl need to be fearful. That goes for little boy abusers and their victims too.

"During that time, I lived in the world of books and fantasy. I put myself to sleep with stories where I was the princess or a heroine. I took my younger brother and sister to the park and the movies and gradually made friends. I loved school even when I was the 'goat.' I was very quiet and subdued in school, but was bratty away from home and school.

"High school was wonderful and terrible. I learned so much and was especially encouraged in my writing classes.

Although we weren't the 'big rods,' I was a part of a great group of friends. We had our arguments, but usually got along together. We attended church, went to movies, swam at the Club, and absolutely abhorred anyone who drank or smoked.

"When high school was over, we all went to college. I went to a liberal arts university right in the city. The rules were different then. I think those rules were my lifesaver. Even though we did a lot of illegal drinking, 'getting drunk' was still frowned upon, and my older brother kept an eagle eye out to make sure I didn't get too outrageous.

"I loved my student teaching and was so thrilled to be finally having my own class. Since I'd taken a semester off to work, I graduated midyear and started the most awful semester of my teaching career in January. I had forty-three students and a witch for a principal.

"Drinking became my tranquilizer. On Mondays, my friends and I would go to a drive-in movie with a six-pack of beer and out on Friday afternoons to party before the weekend. That was my excuse for drinking that year.

"The next year I was fortunate enough to return to the school where I had student taught. I loved teaching and kids all over again, but I didn't stop drinking. Now I was rebelling against being a 'good' girl, and partying was important to me. I didn't like hangovers, but they went away quickly.

"My dad found an article about overseas teaching. I applied, filled out those detailed government forms, and was accepted. My sister typed the forms for me, but I had to fill them out again once I arrived in Germany.

"Glamorous, thrilling, exciting? Yes it was all that and more. Can you imagine a 'nice' Hoosier girl (we were 'girls' in those days) from the conservative state of Indiana suddenly plopped down in the world of jet pilots, missile threats, and beer call? There were wine fests along the

Mosel, the Octoberfest in Munich, and skiing in Garmish There were parties, dances, and trips to Paris and Vienna. It was wonderful! But I was well on my way to becoming, or I already was, an alcoholic.

"Of course I fell in love, and he was a great guy, but he drank as much, if not more, than I did. I know he went to law school and married, but I don't know if he ever quit drinking. I looked up his name in the telephone book once when I was in his city after I retired, but didn't call.

"I returned to Indiana and finished my Master's Degree in guidance and counseling. I'd broken up with my true love and couldn't stand Indiana even though I'd been very homesick while I was in Germany. I headed to Denver for two years, and here, I think, was where my closet drinking started.

"I also did a lot of drinking and driving, which was not only stupid, but also so wrong. Suppose I'd killed or maimed someone. My dad died in November of that first year in Denver. He was in his early sixties. I don't know what the death certificate said, but alcoholism was certainly a part of it. I still miss him—my sober father. I loved him even when he was intoxicated, but I don't miss those times.

"I decided to apply for overseas teaching again. This time it wasn't so glamorous. It was a naval base in Newfoundland—a rugged, wild and beautiful place. About this time, the pill emerged and changed a lot of attitudes about sex—including mine. I fell in love again and when his plane crashed, I cried for two weeks before I let anyone know. But I also drank for those two weeks. I truly was grieving, but again I was using alcohol as a crutch.

"I had a wonderful year teaching in England. If I had to choose a city to live in, it probably would be London. There is so much to do there, and it's a walking city. However, I would need a much higher income to live comfortably there.

"Now I applied for teaching in Alaska, and I wound up at a naval base out on the Aleutian chain. Another year of partying and drinking, and I managed to get myself involved with a married man. I'd always been so contemptuous of the women who got involved with the class B bachelors (married with wife and kids back at home base,) but I did the whole bit—just as some of my friends had done.

"Of course, that fizzled when he went back to his home base. Then I went to Kodiak, Alaska—the island terrific in the North Pacific—and it is. I wish I could say I quit drinking then, but I didn't. There was no big romance in those years—just a few short-lived liaisons. By that time, I don't think I really wanted romance. I wanted to drink. I drank more and more by myself. I was careful to not drink too much when I was at parties or in public, but I sure put it away at home.

"My younger brother died from bladder cancer about that time. I still couldn't see where I was heading, or maybe I did, but just denied it. I kept quiet when people talked about alcoholism. Drugs made their appearance. I never got into that, but if I'd been a little younger, I would have been a true believer in flower power and LSD.

"Did people know how much I drank? No one ever said they did, but I'm sure they were aware of it. There were a few snide remarks, but I just ignored them. I started playing with the idea of quitting the drinking, but those thoughts didn't last long. I did think that maybe I would after I retired and didn't have all the stress of teaching. HA! That was what my mother would call a pipe dream, and I just now made the connection of that phrase with opium.

"How did I function in those years? I had lots of friends. I was a responsible member of society, but how I survived, I don't know. Teaching, my friends and family, and the kids are probably what kept me from giving in and becoming a bag lady. Strangely enough, I did fear that, even though at times, the bag lady life tempted me as a solution to my problems

"At first, retirement was wonderful, I went on three guided hiking trips in England and had a great time. I didn't drink as much. I couldn't and face the hike the next day. But one day, I stayed at the inn and drank all by myself.

"Then I went back to Indiana. That was fine, but I no longer knew people, and it was hard making friends again. I started swimming and met some great people at the Y. I don't think they knew how much I drank at home. I tried real estate selling and tour directing. I didn't like either of those, and I was to the point where I'd rather be drinking anyway.

"Then, as it's put in A.A., I did another geographic: I headed for Oregon. I was thinking a little more seriously about quitting. I knew I was miserable, but how could I give up my alcohol, my best friend? I arrived in Florence, Oregon, in early May 1989, found a place to live, and kept right on drinking. I did go to the library and read the 'Big Book' of Alcoholics Anonymous. I walked all over town. I checked the newspapers and drove around to see if I could find the meeting place.

"Then I went home and drank some more. A movie was on TV about Bill Wilson, the founder of A.A. I bought a gallon of wine and settled down to watch it. I passed out before it was finished.

"I spent the next day again walking everywhere in Florence. I changed my mind over and over, but finally on May 25, 1989, I announced to the Monday night meeting of A.A. that I was an alcoholic. A weight rolled off my shoulders. My troubles didn't end then, but it was a start to a much happier and honest life.

"Coastal Writers welcomed me. Lane Community College at Florence, Oregon, invited me to present a seminar about tour escorting. ***** taught me how to write a book proposal, and I wrote a 'how-to book' about tour escorting.

Four years later, I moved to Eugene, Oregon, and lived there for ten years—writing, going to critique groups, and taking writing classes. I wrote a mystery that was rejected by the very best agents, editors, and publishers.

"My mother died at age ninety-seven, but how fortunate we were to have her all those years. I was very depressed and started going to the Center for Senior Health, both to a group meeting and individual counseling. The Center later invited me to attend a course on being a volunteer senior peer counselor. I finished the course and started doing the counseling. I loved it!

"I kept hearing about the Chemical Dependency Counselor Training Program at Lane Community College, in Eugene, Oregon, and helped to persuade Patricia to enroll. In fact, I wrote one of her recommendation letters. I applied and was accepted. I was the oldest one in my class, but no one ever mentioned age unless I brought it up.

"The hardest thing about the Program for me was the sheer volume of material I had to learn. Even with my background in education and graduate classes in guidance, I had to work and work hard, but I loved it. I learned so much and made such good friends. It was a wonderful Program.

"During the first year, my older brother had a heart attack, and that was a real worry. In June of that year, his daughter, my niece, Sheryl, died suddenly at age 39. That was such a shock.

"I started my internship in the summer, but I wasn't happy, so I resigned in October. However, I still recommend that facility to anyone who asks. My older brother died just before Christmas, and I kept putting off seeking out a new place to finish my intern hours.

"My health suddenly deteriorated, and I realized that I did not want the stresses and strain of being in crisis mode most of the time. My internship convinced me that I didn't want to work for someone else again.

"The idea for this book came to me the summer before I started in the Program. I'd begun a book proposal, but put it away because I just didn't have the time.

"Now I pulled it out again and told my classmates about it and asked for volunteers to let me write their life stories. And here I sit in Florence, Oregon, telling mine. I will never understand why people want to write their memoirs. This is painful, and it's my whole life condensed into about three thousand words.

"There have been so many good things in my life. I've accomplished a lot. I don't like playing 'What If?' But I will always wonder how much more I could have accomplished if I hadn't let alcohol take over my life."

THE LAST WORD

"Since I wrote the book, I get to have the last word or words. I'd intended to write something profound, but that is unnecessary. Simple words have the greatest impact.

"As my critique group read and discussed the stories in this book, I noticed that the many incidents related in this book focused on the negative aspects of our lives. When you talk with my classmates today, you'll notice that even though they don't forget the past, they don't dwell in it.

"They are confident in their abilities and are able to project an understanding and positive attitude to their clients. They develop a close, but professional, relationship with clients. They love life even when life hurls bricks at them. They know they can't save everyone, but they keep trying even when their efforts are greeted with anger, hostility, and indifference. They are definitely heroes!

"Of course, there are times when I'd like to wring some of my classmates' necks, and I know my own neck has been in peril. But they're still my heroes!"

Where Are They Now?

Spring 2005

Angie is working at ***** and loves it. She's thinking about going back to school.

Carsten loves his outdoor job working with teens. He and his wife are expecting a baby soon.

Dawn is working as a counselor at *****. She took some extra hypnotherapy training and has a few clients of her own. She is also researching graduate programs.

Deborah is taking time out to play Grandma, so her daughter can finish college.

Jan is relaxed and happy. This book is off to the publisher.

Joanie is working at a facility that helps women and has acquired her CADC 1.

Jolene is still working at*****, and has assumed guardianship of her grandson. She is thinking about moving, but so far, it's just thinking.

Krista earned her CADC 2. She and her family are moving to Reno, Nevada. Krista's excited and promises to send details soon.

LouAnne moved to England. We're hoping for a long Christmas letter.

Marie We haven't been able to contact her, but we hope all is well, and we hear her news soon.

Marty is still working at ***** with teen clients. Her partner graduated from *****. They've added a new dog to their family.

Mike is in graduate school and interning at ***** prison. In 2004, Mike spearheaded the first annual Saint Patrick's Day family celebration in Eugene, Oregon. No drugs or alcohol!

Mira graduated from the University of Oregon. Right now, she is involved with care giving.

Patricia graduated from University of Oregon with high honors and several awards. She and her husband moved to California, and she's just accepted a counseling position at *****.

Paul "Where are you? Please get in touch. We miss you."

Rica is still working near her home. She helped to develop an in-depth program at the jail that is having a high rate of success. She and her husband are working on their house. She too has her CADC 2.

GLOSSARY

A.A. See **Alcoholics Anonymous**.

Al-Anon An organization to help people, involved in the life of a substance abuser, cope and develop their own rewarding lives.

Alcoholics Anonymous Founded by Bill Wilson and Doctor Bob in 1935 as a fellowship of men and women who meet together to attain and maintain sobriety. The only requirement is a desire to stop drinking. For more information write A.A. General Service Office, Box 459, Grand Central Station, New York, NY 101163, or consult your local telephone directory.

Big Book See **SUGGESTED READING.**

Bottom The point at which a person reaches the worst that can happen because of alcohol and drug addiction (e.g., loss of job, negative involvement with legal system, loss of home or family).

CADC 1 See **Certified Alcohol and Drug Counselor 1, Oregon**.

CADC 2 See **Certified Alcohol and Drug Counselor 2, Oregon**.

Certified Alcohol and Drug Counselor 1, Oregon One thousand hours of internship under supervision of a CADC 2, satisfactory completion of required educational units, passing score on state and national examinations.

Certified Alcohol and Drug Counselor 2, Oregon Four thousand hours of alcohol and drug counseling in an approved facility, satisfactory completion of required educational hours, passing score on state and national examinations, successful presentation of a complete case study before a board of examiners.

CO-OP A program of cooperation between organizations and schools to facilitate training in a business or profession.

Country Fair See **Oregon Country Fair**.

Detox See **Detoxification**.

Detoxification A drug therapy protocol for eliminating a drug from the body—usually the first step in alcohol and drug rehabilitation.

Dual Diagnosis A person suffering from substance addiction in addition to being mentally ill.

DUI Driving under the influence.

DWI Driving while intoxicated.

FAE See **Fetal alcohol effects**.

FAS See **Fetal alcohol syndrome**.

Fetal alcohol effects Same as **Fetal alcohol syndrome** except physical characteristics are not obvious in the affected child.

Fetal alcohol syndrome Neurological damage and obvious physical characteristics in a child caused by a pregnant woman drinking alcohol.

First step of A.A. Admitting that one is powerless over alcohol and life has become unmanageable. See **Alcoholics Anonymous**.

Lane See **Lane Community College**.

Lane Community College A two-year college in Eugene, Oregon, with satellite campuses in smaller communities.

LCC See **Lane Community College**.

N.A. See **Narcotics Anonymous**.

Narcotics Anonymous A nonprofit fellowship of men and women who meet regularly to help each other remain clean. (no drugs)

GED See **General Educational Development**.

General Educational Development Alternate program to completing four years of secondary schooling.

Oregon Country Fair The Oregon Country Fair was started in 1969 and has a rich varied history of alternative art and performance promotion opportunities. It is held near Veneta, Oregon, on three days in the summer. At one time, it was associated with drugs, alcohol, and bizarre behavior. Now it is drug and alcohol free and a family oriented celebration of the arts.

Oregon Health Plan A medical plan for low income uninsured Oregon residents.

Practicum See **CO-OP.**

Rapid Eye Therapy A therapy based on the conscious effort to replicate the rapid eye movement stage of sleep.

Recovery State of being continuously sober and clean from drugs. Recovery is considered an on-going process and involves life changes and spiritual development.

Rogers, Carl Psychologist, instrumental in development of nondirective psychotherapy. He stressed unconditional positive regard, genuineness, and empathic understanding in creating a positive interaction with a client.

San Felipo syndrome A progressive, degenerative, and terminal disease with cognitive delay. It attacks the internal organs primarily the liver and kidneys. (Krista has assumed guardianship of her sister. "At thirty-five she has outlived the life expectancy of twelve to sixteen years." Krista writes. "Sadly her life consists of a feeding tube, diapers and no recognition of anything. She also has no voice and is unable to communicate It's difficult to see someone you love experience life this way.")

Sponsor In twelve-step programs, a person with past history of addiction or other problems who helps facilitate a person's recovery from addiction.

Sponsor In the military, the active duty member of the family who sponsors his dependents—especially in overseas assignments

Twelve steps of A.A. Twelve steps to creating a sober and rewarding life. See **Alcoholics Anonymous**.

Twelve-step programs Alternate programs, such as Overeaters Anonymous, which are based on the twelve-step organization of Alcoholics Anonymous.

Work-study See **CO-OP**.

IF YOU WANT TO BE A SUBSTANCE ABUSE COUNSELOR

Visit rehabilitation facilities. See if they have a good internship program: continuing education, direct contact with clients, and possibilities for future employment.

Check with your state's certification board for requirements and qualifications.

Research community colleges to find a drug and alcohol counselor training program.

As you research the community colleges, think about possible enrollment at a four-year college in this or a related field.

Then ask yourself these questions.

"Am I able to handle the paperwork?"

"Am I able to work in 'crisis' mode?"

"Am I willing to start at the bottom?"

"Do I genuinely care for people?"

"Do I realize that social contact with clients must be kept to an absolute minimum?"

"Do I understand about self-care and burnout?"

"Can I maintain confidentiality?"

"Can I maintain the line between counselor and client without sacrificing the client's best interest?"

"Can I refrain from imposing my beliefs and judgments on the client?"

"Can I respect a client's ethnic, social, and religious culture?"

Think hard and long about your decision. Then give it a try.

Again, if you have questions or observations, please, e-mail me at jettjg@carrollsweb.com.

SUGGESTED READING

Alcoholics Anonymous, *Big Book*, Third edition, (Alcoholics Anonymous World Services, 1989) 575p

Corey, Gerald, *Theory and Practice Of Counseling and Psychotherapy,* Sixth edition (Wadsworth/Thompson Learning, 2001) 556p ISBN 0-534-34823-8

Inabs Darryl S., Pharm.D. and William E. Cohen, *Uppers, Downers, And All Arounders,* Fourth Edition (CNS Publications, 2000) 493p ISBN 0-926544-26-8

A reliable source (and you know who you are) has informed us that the state and national test creators glean most of questions in the state and national certification test from the books written by Corey and Inabs that are listed above.

WEB SITES

Addiction Research Foundation: **http://www.ash.or**

Al-Anon: **www.al-anon.org**

Alcoholics Anonymous: **www.aa.org**

Center For Substance Abuse Treatment:
http://www.samhsa.gov/csat/csta.htm

Center on Addiction and Substance Abuse (CASA):
http://www.casacolumbia.org/home.htm

Narcotics Anonymous: **www.na.org**

National Clearing House For Alcohol and Drug Information:
http://ww.health.org/

National Clearing House on Families and Youth:
http://www.acf.dhhd.gov/programs/fysb

There are many more sources of information and help, but I was unable to list them here. You will find links as you search the web.

Made in the USA
Monee, IL
05 November 2026

67947707R10109